DOWN FROM THE MOUNTAINTOP

Down
from the
Mountaintop

*From Belief to
Belonging*

JOSHUA DOLEŽAL

University of Iowa Press   *Iowa City*

University of Iowa Press, Iowa City 52242

Copyright © 2014 by Joshua Doležal

www.uiowapress.org

Printed in the United States of America

Design by Barbara Haines

The University of Iowa Press is a member of Green Press Initiative and is committed to preserving natural resources.

Printed on acid-free paper

ISBN-13: 978-1-60938-239-1
ISBN-10: 1-60938-239-0
LCCN: 2013952703

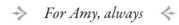 *For Amy, always*

CONTENTS

Author's Note

To protect others' privacy I have occasionally altered minor details and changed or omitted names. I have conceded most factual corrections suggested by family and friends except for a few cases where my memory differs from theirs. To remember is to reconstruct and interpret, and this is as truthful a story as my memory can tell.

If there were a road back to the Montana of my childhood, it would be heavy with rain. The pavement would wind out of Missoula past the old highway cafes, westward through Arlee and Plains, beyond Thompson Falls, Trout Creek, Noxon, then a sharp turn north into the Bull River Valley, where the river is sometimes a marsh. It would be early spring, when the streams churn with the earth, when rejoicing and weeping are one torrent spilling over the banks and there is no telling the shallows from the deeps.

I imagine the road climbing out of the valley to skirt Bull Lake, where a butte rises several hundred feet above the far shore, its image snaking over the water. The surface of the lake ripples in the rain. Dark fir trees flank the highway, light moss in their boughs, dead grass lying matted against the sides of the ditch. A deer bolts from the brush, turns tail, and bounds away.

Then it comes, the long descent into Troy—the huge gravel pit above Lake Creek and the cottonwood trees rising over the town. The chain-link fence around the road graders. The trailer court. The motel and the grocery store. The wide curve along the softball fields, the high school track, and the chipped yellow goalposts. The old wooden grandstand and the railroad tracks and a train rattling through. The caboose. The thump of the tracks, then Riverside Avenue down to the one-lane bridge with its wooden planks. The iron trestle crowned by an osprey's nest. The Kootenai River below. A log passing beneath the planks on the steely water.

Across the bridge a few miles out of town, the road climbs above an old farm along the river. The forest grows thick once more, the slope launching straight out of the valley. Gravel roads veer off into the trees, the main road climbing, long sightlines opening over the valley. A logged timber plot appears, then an overgrown apple orchard, and, at last, the driveway angling up a steep grade to the unfinished house with its cedar shingles and tar-papered walls and the large windows overlooking the way back to my home. No matter how many years have passed, whenever I remember those windows streaked with a gunmetal sky, a cold front of lament sweeps over me, and even the clearest day grows dark.

Sunset. The red hem of sky is frayed by treetops. I am eight years old. From the living room of my home, I look out across a steep valley. The mountain to the south is patched with old clearcuts. The profile of the ridge cuts across the pale sky to the west, and I can see the boundary where the old growth shears off from the brush, baring the lumpy scalp of the mountain. A train whistle rises from deep in the valley like a birdcall.

I sit on the sofa. The room is full of people bowed in prayer. My father leans forward in his wooden rocker, bracing his elbows on the armrests. Many men sit on the edges of their metal folding chairs, their foreheads wrinkled. Some hide their faces in their hands. The women have crossed their arms over their stomachs and some have covered their heads with white linen cloths. Others let their long hair fall into their laps. My mother bends at a weathered upright piano, her cheeks nearly touching the yellow keys. Above her head a thick rack of elk antlers is mounted to the cedar paneling. In the corner between my father and mother a steel lamp hangs by a chain from the ceiling. A circle of light glows above the lamp. The room is silent but for a few murmurs, the nasal hiss of a man's breath, and the creak of the chairs.

In truth my own eyes are closed. The view from the window, the shape of the lamp on the wall, such are the flights my thoughts take during these long ceremonies when others seem so sure of themselves. Remembering this scene now I want to embrace the whole room, the valley outside, the mountain, the sky. I want the big picture this time, not the guilt I felt as a child when my mind could not see what the others believed. I want—impossibly—to acknowledge those men and women without judgment.

My parents are young and filled with evangelical zeal. My father is short and stocky with the thick beard of his Czech relatives, his face deeply tanned after a summer of gardening. He has the look of a man rarely in doubt. Though my mother's eyes are closed, I know their soft fire. In this memory my parents seem younger than I have ever been, truly convinced that their lives rest on bedrock. Looking back, part of me wants their unwavering hope. I cannot dismiss the fact of their belief, that a whole roomful of people can shut their eyes to nightfall and flesh-colored sky and fall silent, knowing nothing but the impressions of their varied internal worlds, yet nearly leaning out of their chairs toward the thought of one vision, one need.

If you were to ask these men and women what creed they follow, they would say they go where the Spirit leads. Ask them to define this Spirit, they might speak of the groundswell of faith in San Francisco when hippies began calling themselves the Jesus People, touting radical Christian faith. Some of the men and women in this room would remember similar groups cropping up in Seattle, branching out along the highways and dirt roads to small towns like Troy. My parents would remember this. They would remember Bob Dylan joining the ranks, singing "Saved," "Slow Train," "Shot of Love." They would recall the paradox of the devout hipster returning to the land while trying to rise above it, his shoulder-length hair and unruly beard the marks of one set apart. But there are no leaders here, no priests, just one creed: that each one strains to hear a small voice within, a whisper somewhere beneath the noise.

A boy thinking of trees and the faded sky, a boy who longs to step out into the night, I am alone in this heavy silence of belief.

———

In the dark the ridge has merged with the sky. Pinpricks of stars arc above the silhouettes of trees. Dew soaks through my shirt as I lie on the lawn after slipping away from the crowd. The windows above me glow as I listen to the muffled rumble of talk through the walls. A branch snaps deep in the woods behind the house. A squirrel chatters. I think of the apples in the orchard a dozen yards away, imagining a bear as black as the night snuffling out onto the lawn. My pulse quickens. I picture myself leaping to my feet, dashing toward the sliding glass door to the basement, the bear closing the gap. Blood thuds in my temples as I lie still, breathing, making peace with what I cannot know.

After a moment I stand and walk down the slope of the lawn toward the row of aspens and birch along the road. The edge of the lawn drops into a ditch. I follow the familiar footholds down the bank to a birch ringed by strips where, as a younger child, I peeled away the tree's bark. A half moon shimmers through the branches. I begin to climb.

Near the top the tree narrows enough for me to hold the trunk between my thighs. I have to stretch to reach the next branch. I find handholds on both sides of the trunk, clenching my belly as I begin to shinny up. When my chin is almost level with my hands, I grope for the next branch. My body brushes the trunk. The moon throbs in the ribs of the tree. My knees search for a grip, sliding over the smooth bark. The branches bite into my palms as I press against the curve of the wood. My body shivers and burns. I strain to hear this rising voice, this tight spiral of heat. My eyes fix on the edge of the moon. A truck coughs to a start in the driveway. I freeze as the headlights sweep over me. The others begin leaving, car doors slamming, engines firing. Before long I am alone in the dark, high in the branches of the birch tree, clinging to my first taste of belief.

———————

The next morning. Rivulets stream down the windows as I sit at the table with my family, the road outside glistening through the blackened branches like a slug in dead grass. *Oh that my head were waters, and mine eyes a fountain of tears, that I might weep day and night.* My father reads from the book of Jeremiah. The cover of his Bible is made of tanned elk hide that my mother sewed into the binding after cutting away the commercial hardback. Shame slithers along my belly as I listen. *Oh that I had in the wilderness a lodging place of wayfaring men, that I might leave my people and go from them, for they be an assembly of treacherous men.* My sister studies her hands in her lap. Her face is a shadow. Pale light washes through the window over her neck. Wisps rise from her hair. They are the color of the light. My mother sits across from my sister. The skin of her face is the color of bones. She gazes out into the rain as my father reads. *Take heed every one of his neighbor, and trust not in any brother: for every brother will utterly supplant, and every neighbor will walk with slanders. And they will deceive every one his neighbor, and will not speak the truth.* My father bends over the book, one side of his face pale, the other obscured. His voice has the creak of old wood, though he is still young. His thick hair and beard are walnut-toned, the sweep of his brow as smooth as freshly tilled earth. *For the mountains will I take up a weeping and wailing, and for the habitations of the wilderness a lamentation, because they are burned up, so that none can pass through them.* I shiver as I remember the birch bark scraping my palms. For a moment I think my father can sense my guilt. But his forehead is so smooth. He seems to hear no more than the rhythm of the words, as if this wave of lament washing over me cannot touch him—as if he is an old river stone.

Was he always? Glancing through his Bible once, I was surprised to find nearly every passage highlighted or underscored multiple times, with occasional exclamatory notes. It was the palimpsest of his mind as a much younger man, when he wrote my mother twice a day from Seattle, where he had begun speaking in tongues. I have seen photos of him then with shaggy hair, a purple silk shirt with pearl snaps, and sandals on his feet. He is always beaming in those old Polaroids, his shirt lying open over a brushy chest, his face glowing with discovery.

Why must I doubt him now as I recall the jeremiads at the breakfast table that he read so unflinchingly? I want to believe in those days when he was tireless—caught up in the blue sky of his time—when my mother dressed my sister and me in homemade corduroy overalls and plaid shirts with elk-antler buttons and the four of us went to church, where the other Jesus People struck up folk tunes on their guitars. Because if I were to believe in those days, I might believe that I am my father's son, that there is still time for me to realize he has been right all along and I am merely a foolish, wayward boy. This would be a welcome awakening. It is what I have always been groping for with my knifelike words: the hope I might at last say the thing that would reveal me to be so destitute of wisdom that judgment would thunder forth and I would be stricken low enough to repent of my disbelief.

―――――――

Dinnertime, late summer. Many years have passed. Steam rises from fresh rolls on the table, where the dishes hold whipped potatoes, a garden salad of spinach and yellow pear tomatoes, creamed cabbage, and grilled elk steak. As is customary, my father reads an entire Bible chapter before the meal, beginning where he left off the previous day. When he reaches the final page of Revelation, he will begin with the first chapter of Genesis and proceed as before.

His text tonight is the fourth chapter of Deuteronomy, the Old Testament book of law. For my benefit he reads the closing verses of the preceding section, where Moses learns he will not see the Promised Land, but must pass the vision to his successor. *Charge Joshua*, God tells Moses, *and encourage him, and strengthen him: for he will go over before this people, and he will cause them to inherit the land.* My mother gazes out the window as she listens. I know she is praying silently, trying to envision me as my namesake—the firstborn leader of his people—the way she thinks of my sister, Rachel, in relation to the Jewish matriarch who wept for her exiled descendants.

Now therefore listen, O Israel, unto the statutes and unto the judgments which I teach you, that you might live and go in and possess the land which the God of your fathers has given you. I begin to suspect this chapter is not merely the next in my father's daily sequence but rather a deliberate subtext of rebuke. After two degrees and travel abroad, I no longer share my parents' faith. They have resorted to passive messages, sending symbolic birthday gifts such as a shofar, the ram's horn sounded by Jewish priests during holy days, which is meant to remind me of my spiritual destiny. We are not Jewish, yet my parents claim this tradition as part of their faith. Tonight they are hoping that I will hear the message and experience a change of heart.

Only take heed to yourself, and keep your soul diligently, lest you forget the things which your eyes have seen, and lest they depart from your heart all the days of your life: but teach them to your sons and to your sons' sons. A vein rises along the center of my father's forehead as he reads. My mother stares unblinkingly across the table between us. She is still wearing her apron, her hands folded in her lap. Sunlight washes over the tablecloth, raising a sheen on our empty stoneware plates. Fresh yellow tulips glow in the vase at the center of the spread, their stalks suspended in the water, and the whole house is silent but for the words of Moses resonating in the dry baritone of my father's voice. *But the Lord has taken you, and brought you forth out of the iron furnace, even out of Egypt, to be unto him a people of inheritance.*

For a moment I am able to listen only to the rhythm of the language, imagining the light washing over the food as my parents' love made visible. In that instant I am able to overlook the message behind the words. But the stridency of the verses soon grates on my ears, and my father's voice becomes a wave breaking over and over against my face. I cross my arms and turn toward the window, where I can just make out the road through the trees. An engine drones somewhere up the mountain, steadily drawing closer until a flatbed pickup stacked with firewood rattles by and out of sight.

When my father finishes his chapter, we will begin passing the food, buttering the rolls, which will have long since lost their warmth, and spooning the salad onto our plates. The small talk will begin, as it must— my mother's questions about my summer Forest Service job, my pre-recorded replies, the inevitable shift to the subject of war, and the same tired lines. "What should we do, let them kill their own people?" my father will ask, and I will say something about McDonald's restaurants springing up on every street corner we claim to liberate. He will snort and tell me I have my head in the sand. This will infuriate me, and I will put down my fork to tick off on my fingers the ways the United States antagonizes the rest of the world with its military occupations, cultural kitsch, and economic imperialism. He will mutter something about Islam and end-times prophecy: wars, rumors of wars, imminent apocalypse.

Heavy clouds will pass between us, anger flickering over our faces. Sharp words will crack in the air. But these will be foolish words. They will have power only to produce more of their kind. One of us must desist.

———————

I still travel that rainy road of memory—the highway out of Missoula, the north stretch through the marshes of the Bull River Valley, the bridge over the Kootenai. Then the sidehill up the steep mountainside, the evergreens, the valley opening to the west. I imagine the orchard and see my father climbing a ladder into an apple tree, stretching toward the top with his pruning shears. My mother gathers fallen branches from the wet grass, stacking them in a garden cart for the burn pile. From my father's perch he can see the river thousands of feet below, train cars snaking along the rocky shore. He knows who he is, as deeply rooted in his native soil as one of his plum trees. For years I have searched for that certainty, wandering the Tennessee hills, the lowlands of Uruguay, the Idaho wilderness, and the corn-covered plains. By now I know that birth is no guarantee of belonging, that some yearnings long for what never was true. Still, I am thirsty with memory. I keep following that road up the mountain, hoping it will lead me home.

PART ONE

ONE

The Sweet Spot

When I suited up for Little League at age ten, shrugging into a maroon nylon top and pulling on my gleaming white pants rimmed with elastic, I distinguished myself by carrying a wooden bat to the plate. It was a thirty-two-inch Worth cut from a blonde ash tree, and with its thick handle and barrel it likely weighed at least two or three pounds. It was an odd choice for a Little Leaguer, since lightweight metal bats had more pop and far more durability. But I was a purist. Wood was what the pros used, the kind of bat that met the ball with a gut-tingling crack, unlike the ping of aluminum, which sounded more like a sound effect on a video game than a good, honest hit. I knew my bat could break, and every time I caught a pitch off the tip or close to the handle, the vibration stung my hands. But when I found the sweet spot, when a pitch came in at belt level and I got good wood on it, the shock washed over my body like I'd jumped into a lake.

I needed that feeling for more reasons than I could express, and I gave it my whole attention, the way I forgot everything else while eating cherry cheesecake. It was a form of love, that sweet contact, like the bliss I'd seen on other people's faces in church, hands raised skyward, tears streaming down their upturned cheeks. And when I knew the ball would clear the fence, when I saw the pitch fly from the barrel and felt the echo in my chest and *knew*, it was a form of truth.

Baseball was my father's game, one of the few things we had in common and the only exception he made to banning television from our home. Every fall when the World Series began, he borrowed an old black-

and-white set from my grandfather, and we propped it on a chair in the living room, where we fussed with the antennae until the grainy picture snapped into focus. It was there on the brown braided rug, lying on my belly with my chin in my hands, that I watched my team, the Mets, win the 1986 World Series. And two years later on the same tiny screen I saw Kirk Gibson hobble to the plate for the Dodgers, my father's team, and launch a game-winning home run against the Oakland Athletics despite a pulled hamstring and aching knees. For a few moments as Gibson limped around the bases and we jumped on the dining room linoleum to high-five each other, dishes rattling in the cupboard, my father and I were one. He coached each of my teams from the pee wee league through Babe Ruth, managing even the All-Star squads. Every time I stepped to the plate, I could feel him watching from the third-base coach's box, and I wanted to get that feeling back, knowing if I hit a line drive or a long ball, all my errors would be forgiven and he'd give my shoulder a squeeze.

There was no way for me to know when we first began playing catch on our lawn around my fourth birthday that my father was trying to recover something he'd lost. But in the next few years, as I started tee ball and he began grooming me for Little League, I knew he expected more than I could give. He often urged me to throw harder, frustrated by my noodle arm. But arm strength is one of the raw talents only nature bestows, so my earliest memories of catch are laced with a sense of struggle against my body, against myself. Our yard was a steep slope overlooking the Kootenai River Valley west of Troy. An apple orchard and a vegetable garden flanked the lawn, an excellent sledding hill in winter but a poor stand-in for a baseball diamond with its uneven footing. More often than not, I tripped over my own feet while trying to get under a pop fly that my father tossed overhead, losing my bearings while running uphill. The grounders he threw came at me like curveballs, angling downslope as they bounced my way. My errant throws, which increased the more he hollered for me to put some heart into it, usually landed in a bank of tall grass behind the raspberry canes. My father was not a patient man, and the longer it took to hunt for a lost ball the sharper his return throw would be, upping the odds I'd miss it on a short hop and have to chase it down the hill into the ditch, where the birch and aspen trees fronted our country road. No matter how angry we'd get or how many minutes we wasted wading through the grass, we kept at it until dusk, calling it quits when the air began to pulse with crickets and we could no longer see.

I knew these marathon games of catch, though they often felt like failure, were my father's best attempts at love. I would later suit up for football and basketball and even dabble in tennis, but there was never any question that my first loyalty lay with my father's game. It was a gift he wanted to pass on, like his hope of heaven. And when I learned, years later, how my father came to faith as a young man, how he heard the voice of the Holy Spirit and began speaking in angelic tongues, I understood why oiling my glove and lifting my wooden bat from the closet always felt like more than a summer pastime.

When my father was a boy, his world revolved around baseball and his grandfather Adolph, his biggest fan. Adolph was a rough, jolly man who often ate an entire half gallon of Neapolitan ice cream while watching the Dodgers on television and smelled of strawberry, chocolate, vanilla, and Copenhagen snuff when my father kissed him goodnight. They roamed the woods around Libby fishing and hunting, dragging their bounty home to my great-grandmother Sophie, who pressed a nickel into my father's palm for every fish he claimed to have caught and every grouse he said he'd dropped with his grandfather's shotgun. Adolph was also a drinker, sometimes driving home from the fishing hole on the wrong side of the highway, laughing as the oncoming drivers laid on their horns and swerved around him. Even though Adolph didn't make it to many ballgames, when it was summertime and my father ran out to his position at second base, dropping into his infielder's crouch, he hoped to make his grandfather proud.

On the winter day when Adolph died after falling from a ladder in the backyard, my father was far away, struggling to finish his first semester at a junior college in Arizona. He'd followed a high school teammate there to try out for the baseball squad and then maybe find his way to the big leagues, but he did not survive the final cut, and he was still reeling from it when he heard of his grandfather's death. The desert sun baked his face as he walked among blue palm trees in shirtsleeves and sandals, hot tears streaking his cheeks, his chest aching for the emerald water of the

Kootenai River and the craggy rim of the Cabinet Mountains overlooking his home.

When my father came back to Libby that winter, he drifted, working for a spell at the lumber mill, transferring to the community college in Kalispell for a few courses in civil engineering, wandering back to the mill. One evening after work he dropped by a hamburger joint, a place with a pinball arcade where young people gathered to smoke and laugh and nurse milkshakes. The bells on the front door clanked against the glass as he took a seat at the counter, glad for the warmth and the smell of pickles and grease. He recognized a classmate he'd lost touch with, a guy named Kevin who had brought home some friends from Seattle to fix up a van they planned to drive back to the city. They were handsome young men with long hair and beards, and a crowd had gathered around their booth. My father inched closer to listen in. Kevin was talking about the Holy Spirit, reading from a leather Bible lying open on the table. Once he even turned straight to the verse he was looking for, as if the Spirit were guiding his hand.

A few nights later my father sat in Kevin's garage watching the Seattle guys paint the van, an old dairy bus with no side windows. Kevin had invited him to join their commune in the city where they devoted their days to street ministry, but my father wasn't sure. He was making good money at the mill. It seemed reckless to just walk away from a job. He watched Kevin dip a brush in a can of purple paint, scrawling "Jesus Christ" in a giant script over the side of the van. As Kevin stood back to admire it, arms crossed over his chest, my father pointed out that he'd written "Crist" instead of "Christ." The van looked even more hip after Kevin dabbed the missing letter into the curve of the giant C, but my father began to think it might have been a sign. As he sat alone that night praying about whether to go, he felt God speak to him for the first time. *Just like the missing "h,"* he felt a small voice say, *the Holy Spirit is missing from your understanding of me.*

So he hugged his parents goodbye, my grandmother weeping on the front step, and set off for Seattle, where he took an upstairs bunk in the ramshackle commune. During the day my father paced through the city, stopping passersby to ask if he could say a word about Jesus, sometimes jogging alongside them as they tried to hurry away. At night he read the

Bible and prayed alone while the others strummed their guitars, dancing to worship songs in the living room. One evening he was meditating in his bunk upstairs, trying to block out the ruckus below when he felt a peace steal over him, just like the night when he had heard God speak, and suddenly his lips were moving, and he could hear himself whispering in words he did not understand. Then he knew what it was, and he heard a voice again saying *I'm filling you with my Holy Spirit now, and then I will teach you about it in the days ahead.* Now when he opened the Bible the words came alive. He had a testimony, a story to tell. It no longer mattered if he couldn't answer the questions he faced every day on the street. He didn't care if people mocked him for a fool or just lowered their heads and shouldered by. He believed. He had been to the mountaintop, and he had looked over. And he was never again the same.

It took more than thirty years for my father to tell me all this, long after my own journey away from faith was complete. As a boy I knew only that my father wanted me to believe in God the way he wanted me to throw straight and true, firing the ball toward his chest in a tight arc until it snapped in the pocket of his glove. It was something he demanded, a standard I strained to meet. As far as I knew then, he had always been clear-headed and firm. Schooled in the science of land surveying, he seemed more at home with a stack of maps and a calculator than the novels I curled up with under my mother's quilt. I struggled to reconcile my meticulous father, the man who triple-checked his calculations after packing his yellow tripod around the perimeter of a property boundary, with the man who could surrender control of his own tongue and speak in a stream of what sounded like gibberish to me.

Our church was the kind with loud preaching and tambourines jingle-jangling through the worship service. We gathered in an abandoned Forest Service building on a hill overlooking Troy, a space we shared with the Catholic church, which met early in the morning and dispersed an hour before we arrived to set up a hundred metal folding chairs facing a piano and a screen where the words to our worship songs appeared, magnified and bathed in light. It was there I learned about revival meetings where a woman with the gift of tongues might speak in Chinese, not understanding a word coming out of her own mouth, learning after the service that a man from the Sichuan Province had heard God speaking directly to him, in his native dialect, in her voice. It was frightening to imagine the voice of God rumbling through my own vocal chords. It seemed like a superpower, a way for the body to feel proof of what the soul believed. I clapped and sang along with the others, waiting for the Spirit to take possession of me, but this seemed beyond my strength, like the games of catch in the backyard, where I could never quite throw hard enough.

The sermons at the Troy Christian Fellowship were much like my father's coaching, impatient with mediocrity, constantly calling me to higher living. One morning the preacher worked himself into a sweat, pacing before us as if the church were a giant dugout, our buttocks clenched against the hard chairs. There was no stage, and he was not a tall man, but he seemed to tower above us. His text was the book of Exodus, where God delivers the Israelites from bondage in Egypt and calls Moses up Mount Sinai to receive the commandments the people are to live by. "Thou shalt have no other gods before me," the preacher quoted from memory, his voice rising to a shout as he finished the verse, "for I the Lord thy God am a *jealous* God." He stopped to let the words sink in, a vein bulging from his shiny forehead as he stared us down. He went on to tell how even as Moses stood on the mountain receiving the bedrock of Hebrew law directly from the mouth of God, the people grew impatient and melted their own earrings and made a golden calf, which they worshiped as their liberator.

"Imagine," the preacher hissed, his voice fallen into a whisper. "Imagine yourself as a father who has brought up his child in the truth, only to watch him turn away, only to watch him destroy his life at the card table or cast all his passion into gathering riches or grow so proud with learning that he says, 'There is no God.'" The preacher clutched his Bible to his chest and crouched as if he'd caught a hard grounder in the groin.

"You would not give up on that child," the preacher went on, his voice building once more into crescendo, "because the love of a father is a jealous love, jealous for its own flesh and blood the way *God* is jealous for his *chosen* ones, ready to let loose his wrath on them if they waver in what they *know* is the truth."

I looked at the faces around me on Sunday mornings—women weeping with what seemed to be joy, arms raised as they stood swaying to the music, men shouting amens to the other men who marched before us possessed by the Word and the Spirit and the great urgency of sharing the bad news of human nature and the good news of God's chastising rod—and I could not consider myself one of their number, even though I lived in fear for my soul. My father sang with his eyes closed, rocking in his cowboy boots with his hands cupped at his sides as if he were waiting for rain, and my mother pounded out chords on the chipped piano keys. I believed they had a grip on something real, a sensual spirit force that slipped through my fingers and left me feeling empty and cold as I sang the words on the gleaming screen, watching the tambourine player shake her whole body, breasts bobbing beneath her blue paisley dress.

But when I wrapped my hands around the handle of my wooden bat and ripped a pitch into the outfield, the crack echoing down the barrel into my chest, it was like the voice of God in my throat, and my body and spirit flew together down the baseline.

———

When I was old enough for Little League, my father drove me to Libby for that year's draft. Libby sat twenty miles east of Troy, which meant an hour round-trip most weeknights through the summer, but it was worth it because the Libby All-Stars could go all the way to the Little League World Series if they were good enough. Troy had an unsanctioned league where the uniforms featured business names like Acco Cable and ASARCO, the local silver mine. In Libby the teams were named for professional clubs, and the draft for rookies—that year's pool of ten-year-olds—mimicked a major league tryout.

On the day of the draft, all of the coaches gathered at the Libby baseball complex, two adjacent fields sandwiched between the Kootenai River and the railroad tracks. My father and I drove the twenty miles from Troy mostly in silence, my belly awash with excitement when we crunched into the gravel parking lot behind the backstop and joined the crowd. The coaches ran us through the drills, fielding grounders, shagging flies. Then we each got ten swings to show what we could do at the plate. I performed well enough to rate as a top pick, rattling several pitches against the sheet-metal fence in the outfield. As in the major leagues, the worst team had first dibs in the draft, and I was dismayed to learn by the end of the evening that I'd been chosen by the Mets. But once I met my teammates for practice, a group of scrawny boys nearly all smaller than me, I accepted my fate. Though my father played for the Dodgers in Little League and had rooted for them ever since, I searched the box scores every day for Dwight Gooden and Darryl Strawberry and Ray Knight, counting the days to the postseason, when my grandfather would lend us the little black-and-white box and I'd get to watch the pros at home.

My mother grew up without a television, and when she and my father married, living in a tipi for a year before building a house on the land they purchased on a mountain overlooking Troy, they shared a vision of home as a refuge from the outside world. My sister was born there, delivered by my father, as I had been. In our living room the couch and the wooden rocking chair faced the piano, an upright in the German style with braces beneath the keyboard, a thick back panel, and a heavy lid made for holding flowers or clocks or lamps for reading sheet music. The hallway on the main floor featured an inset bookcase, which held the Encyclopedia Britannica Great Books collection and my mother's eclectic library, Chaim Potok's *The Chosen*, Kenneth Grahame's *The Wind in the Willows*, James Herriot's *All Creatures Great and Small*. My father read the newspaper and the Bible and considered other reading frivolous, rousting me from my bedroom to pull weeds when I lounged there too long with a book. Baseball was the one crack in the fortress, the one out from garden chores, the only excuse for television to invade the protective bubble of faith and homegrown food and music my parents had created for us.

The God I heard about each Sunday might have considered baseball a golden calf I worshipped every summer on the field and every fall in front of the television set. And there were times when the spitting and crotch scratching cast a frown over my mother's face. But baseball was an open door to the world my father allowed, one vestige from his past he did not surrender to the new life on the homestead. So I was allowed to worship the game in my own way, plastering the cement walls of my basement bedroom with photographs of Mookie Wilson and Keith Hernandez and Lenny Dykstra clipped from my grandfather's *Sports Illustrated* magazines. As I lay on my bed gazing at the wall mosaic of my heroes, I dreamed of one day making it to The Show. And because I learned most of what I knew about baseball from my father, this was much like my trust in heaven, though I gave no thought to the irony of a game—a worldly pleasure—sating my yearning for redemption.

Baseball followed Pentecostal doctrine to a surprising degree. Every game, like a church service, began with a song. The true believers were not content to sit idly by in the bleachers. When we were down they hollered encouragement, and when we were up, boy, they banged on the aluminum bleachers and stomped their feet and carried on like they'd got good religion.

One tenet of Pentecostal belief was immediate revelation, the idea that God could speak directly to the individual through spiritual gifts. Speaking in tongues was the most dramatic of these, but my parents believed there were Christians with the gift of miraculous healing, the gift of interpreting what others were saying in tongues, the gift of prophecy, the gift of teaching, and many others. Every time I scooped a grounder or steadied myself beneath a fly ball, it was only to get one out closer to my next at bat, when I could dig into the batter's box and let my true gift shine. "Don't leave your light under a bushel," as one verse said, and I strove to obey that command every time I lowered myself into my stance. Everywhere else on the field I was above average—decent speed, an adequate arm, steady with the glove. At the plate I was unique, often batting above .700 for the regular season, launching pitches well beyond the two-hundred-foot fences. Our preacher described spiritual gifts as a believer's full inheritance, recounting how he had prayed for the gift of healing, asking God for his full reward. In church I knew I'd come up short. But on the diamond, the sacred ground I shared with my father, I came into that reward.

Baseball is a team effort, but it is just as much an individual discipline, each fielder enisled in his own thoughts, each batter standing alone at the plate. The solitary togetherness of the sport resonated with the stamina I'd gained from sitting through two-hour revival meetings and with the inner space I'd been encouraged to explore through prayer. Reading was also an outgrowth of that life, and writing would later fulfill a similar urge to the reaching out of prayer, the questioning and the crying out and the inner groping for peace. As a child nothing made more sense to me than batting, where my father might be watching from the third base line, and my mother and grandparents might be cheering from the stands, but no one else could take my place between the chalk lines of the batter's box. It was a meditative place where I stood in a half crouch awaiting the pitcher's delivery, my back elbow cocked to keep my swing level, hands gripping the handle without squeezing too much, my whole body coiled and ready. The pitcher faded in my vision, the chatter from the infielders dimmed, and I waited to see the ball in flight, my legs and arms tightening in the split second before I decided to swing.

I played by instinct, by the sudden knowledge of whether a pitch was too high or too low or whether it was slicing in straight across the plate, belt high, in my wheelhouse. When that happened, when I felt the pitch arcing toward the sweet spot, my body twisted forward to meet the ball, arms whipping the wooden bat, eyes fixed on the blur of the pitch. There was a power rising within me, a spirit force welling up. This was my gift. This was my full inheritance.

———————

As a child I felt these things without naming them, buoyed or weighed down by sudden impressions of joy or guilt. The elation on my face when the shock of the sweet spot rippled up my arms into my chest surely appeared to everyone else as a kid having fun, but the feeling resonated with me as proof of God's favor, though I could not have explained why. Eric Liddell, the pious sprinter in *Chariots of Fire*, captured it when he said, "God made me for a purpose, but he also made me fast. And when I run I feel his pleasure." So when the game went badly, when I let a grounder skip between my legs or fisted a pitch into an easy pop fly, a pall fell over my spirits not unlike the nagging fear that my soul was in peril.

The morning after a game, my father would have forgotten the outcome, good or bad, but I had more difficulty letting go and often sat at the breakfast table in a brooding silence. He tried to make me laugh then, cracking jokes about how it took more energy to frown than to smile, but this only pushed me deeper into gloom, and if I sometimes poured too much huckleberry syrup on my pancakes, it was only as a stand-in for my next chance to step up to the plate and make sweet contact once more.

When I launched a home run and circled the bases with the echo of it still tingling in my hands, my father often said, perhaps to curb my pride, "You're only as good as your next at bat." I took this to heart. It was a literalism I was internalizing in church, a way of sorting the world into the clean and the unclean, trusting rituals of penance to make me whole. Like a prayer for forgiveness, which might wash away my sin for that instant, every trip to the plate was a mountaintop where I could not linger, an absolution pitching me back into the valley to climb out again. To my shame I can scarcely remember my teammates, so intent I was on claiming the game as my one true gift, sitting alone in a packed dugout with my wooden bat at my side. Sometimes I held it at arm's length, studying the waves of the wood grain rippling beneath the blue Worth logo, then twisting the handle and closing one eye so I could track the straight lines of the side grain toward the sweet spot in the middle of the barrel, the place where I belonged, where I wanted to live my whole life.

TWO

The Shadow of the Kootenai

Sunday morning. Late September. A rusted station wagon coughs to a stop near the ballpark in Troy with its wooden grandstand and flaking green paint. Pickup trucks and minivans line the street behind the bleachers, where a clutch of people stand shivering in the wind. It is a cloudy day and the chill sweeping down from the high country promises that winter is on its way.

Cliff Olson, the worship leader, has summoned us to the field as the finale to a prayer vigil we've been holding for weeks. Each morning for the past month I heard my parents rise in the dark, boards creaking over my head as they knelt beside their bed, murmurs drifting down to me through the floor. Now the entire congregation—the whole Troy Christian Fellowship—has gathered in the street, fifty or sixty strong, ready to wave flannel banners spelling out Romans 3:23, "For all have sinned and fallen short of the glory of God," and 1 Corinthians 13:8, "Love never fails." We are to reenact the Battle of Jericho, when Joshua and the Israelites marched around the enemy city, blowing their horns until the walls fell down. We are to take our little town for Christ. I am thirteen and embarrassed to be here, my hands drawn into the sleeves of my sweatshirt, shoulders hunched against the cold as I gaze at the timbered ridges encircling the town, imagining the mountains as the great walls of Jericho.

A few dented trumpets appear in the crowd, holdovers from defunct high school pep bands. We look like the ghosts of a homecoming parade. Cliff blows on his hands as he tunes his blue Ovation, ready to play praise songs to keep our spirits high. He is a tall, dark man with the good looks of a gunslinger, and I admire the pearl frets built into the neck of his guitar. As he strums a chord, fussing with the tuning pegs, I feel a little less ashamed to be standing here with my family. My father is humming to himself as we wait. My mother prays silently, her chin tucked into the top of her coat. I know she imagines herself doing battle in the heavenly realm. My sister clutches a small banner she made of old corduroy and wool, her cheeks reddened by the wind. She has my mother's blond hair and my father's face, and she is still too young to doubt them. But I'm wondering why we can't stay in church like everyone else. Why must we march through the streets? I decide to stick close to Cliff, as if the nearer I am to his guitar the less ridiculous I'll be.

Across the railroad tracks, hidden by a stand of birch and fir trees, runs the Kootenai River. On another day we might gather there for a baptism, watching the minister draw a trembling soul under the water and bring her back sputtering and praising God. A revival preacher once offered a homily on the banks of the Kootenai that I find myself dreaming all over again as I wait for the march to begin.

The river is grace, the preacher said, *the grace of the grave. All the old habits fall away beneath the surface of the water—all anger, all lust, all unclean things fall away. And when we rise up out of that shadowy grave, and when we walk out of the water with the stench of that old life dropping from us like the smell of weeds rotting along the shore—hallelujah—then we are bound for streets of gold. Behold,* he said, *when dead things pass away, all things become new.*

I shiver as I remember the green water lapping against the stones, the rocking moss, the darkness farther out beneath the current. Cliff snaps me from my reverie with an opening chord, and a shout goes up as the crowd lurches forward along the railroad tracks. Two blocks away stands the ramshackle fence at the Home Bar where loggers and miners chewed up the grass with their boots the night before, dancing to the last outdoor band of the year. The heathens. The Sodomites and drunkards. I know we have come to wage war on that crowd. Soon we are singing the old spiritual about Jericho, Cliff strumming in my direction as if I have the power to raise my arms and convert the whole town. My father claps a hand on my back and I stride ahead with the others, trying to look more certain than I feel.

24

Pentecostalism in my family began with my great-grandfather J. L. Mussell, who homesteaded in the sagebrush near Nampa, Idaho, and pastored an Assembly of God church where sheep ranchers and sugar-beet farmers and their hired men gathered. One of them was my grandfather Rupert, a lean and handsome man, dark from long days in the sun. He was a veteran of the Second World War, when he served with the Merchant Marines in the Pacific Theater. Searching for quiet on a sheep ranch in Idaho after the war, he happened upon the country church and fell in love with one of J. L.'s daughters, Dorcas, a young woman whose curly hair and bright smile must have won her many suitors before she caught Rupert's eye.

Southern Idaho was a landscape of crushing heat, howling winter winds, snow drifting as deep as ten or twelve feet—the kind of country that backed a poor man up against his clapboard walls. Those who found no solace in whiskey wanted their religion to have a little kick when they gathered every Sunday. The foot stamping and clapping during the worship time, the shouted amens in a deep baritone helped a man feel the blood burning in his hands and feet, the rumble of his own voice proof he was still alive.

My mother was born out in the sagebrush before my grandfather took a seasonal job with the Forest Service in Libby, fighting fires through the summer and fall, mopping floors at the local hospital through the winter. Libby was a thriving town, flush with timber, but the family was poor, so they often knelt in the living room before bed as my grandfather prayed for steady work. He found a permanent job in the Forest Service soils lab, where he tested samples and watched for wildfires, when he could earn enough overtime to bring home a treat of orange juice or cottage cheese. All my mother knew as a child was the razor edge of want. She remembered the howling desert winds, and those years of yearning set her apart from other children. As she became a young woman, she needed to burn brighter, fan her flames higher.

So when the revivals came to Libby my mother was hungry for renewal. She was slender, scarcely five feet tall, her gaze unflinching, her back as straight as a larch tree. She was fifteen, learning Joan Baez songs on a Sears guitar, reading Thoreau, embroidering daisies and shooting stars on her white blouses. It was the year of Dylan's album *New Morning* and Van Morrison's *Moondance*. The revival preachers seemed to be speaking directly to her as they spoke of feeding every day on God's Word. "Come get fresh bread," they cried, their Bibles held high. And she began searching the scriptures as never before, feeling them awaken to her.

Now she had a testimony, and when my mother saw young people flocking to faith, she knew someone had to help them find their way. So she gathered a few others to petition the principal at Libby High for a gathering place on school grounds where they could meet during the lunch hour to pray. And this was how she met my father, who had come home from Seattle newly baptized and eager to spread his good news. When the student group met with the principal, my father came in support, a grin spreading between his handlebar moustache and soul patch as he introduced himself to a young woman who seemed like sunshine itself, her golden hair falling in two braids beside her cheeks.

My parents' radiance softened the principal as he gazed at them through his horn-rimmed glasses. He was unmanned by their innocence, the absence of guile in their smiles. These weren't the day-trippers who kept him up nights. These were mere babes. So he leaned over his desk and gave them permission to gather in the school library at noon as long as they kept their noise down. He smiled as they each shook his hand and filed out of his office. And I wonder if I have that man to thank in part for my life, if my mother and father would have fallen so quickly in love if they had not been sealed by that small victory.

They courted for a few years while my mother finished high school and my father went back to his civil engineering courses, writing to her nearly every day. My father wrote in tiny capital letters, every line like the text of a map legend, punctuated freely by exclamation marks. My mother's hand was a free and looping script with lupine and larkspur drawn in the margins. In place of her name, she sometimes drew a rising sun.

When they married in early June at a park down the street from my father's home, they were dressed all in white, my father wearing a shirt with an open butterfly collar, my mother walking to meet him in a handmade dress, wild rose blossoms woven into her hair. That summer they lived in a tipi made of canvas panels that my mother stitched on my grandmother's sewing machine. With their faith blazing strong, my parents thought nothing could go wrong.

But after summer turned to fall, my mother miscarried and nearly hemorrhaged to death. She wanted no meddling doctors, no false priests. If it was God's will she should die, then so it must be. My mother grew so weak she could no longer open her eyes, her jaw fallen slack and ashen. She recalls lying beneath a bloodstained blanket, right up against the void, ready to yield if it was her time.

Once she came back to herself, she believed God gave her a personal poem, to remember what it meant to survive the shadow of death. It was Psalm 116: "The cords of death entangled me, the anguish of the grave came over me.... The Lord protects the unwary; when I was brought low he saved me." This was epiphany, the mountaintop every revival meeting labored to reach, the legacy I was born into a year after my mother's health returned.

This was why she named me Joshua, meaning "God of Salvation," for the leader who gathered his people and said, "Choose you this day whom you will serve.... But as for me and my house, we will serve the Lord." Once I bore this name, my mother believed my destiny was sealed by an unbreakable covenant. Every revival fanned this hope aflame. And so leaving my mountain home as a young man felt like walking away from the truth, exiled from the Promised Land.

When I marched into Troy that September morning with my father's hand on my back and my eyes on Cliff's guitar, I was trying mightily to live up to my name. The doubts churning in my belly could not be real. Surely the faith etched into my mother's countenance was the truth. Yet I would discover years later that the lesson of Jericho was not salvation. The biblical Joshua burned the entire city, sparing no one but the harlot Rahab, who had hidden the Hebrew spies sent ahead of the army. My namesake spoke a curse over the ashes of the fallen city, damning any who would try to rebuild it with the loss of their firstborn and youngest sons. We could not possibly have meant what we were singing as we marched into Troy: "Joshua fit de battle of Jericho, Jericho, Jericho, Joshua fit de battle of Jericho, and the walls came a-tumblin' down ..." There was hope in the crowd, though, real desire.

I have long since ceased my imitations of prayers, but that old revival feeling still smolders in my blood. Every time I turn north of Missoula into the mountains, into the thick fir forest where the Clark Fork and the Bull River flow, my body wakes to the wail of wind down a steep mountain ridge, the ache of loss, the fear of exile. The blue mood sweeping over me when I think of Troy is grief for a place I love, a growing sense that much of it was never mine.

It was the very sadness that chilled my chest as I paraded through town with the others waving their banners, Cliff sawing away at his chords. As we soldiered down Bar Street singing and clapping, my courage failed me and I hid my face beneath my hood, my gut knotted with desire and shame. When I lifted my eyes, I met the gaze of a woman standing behind a storm door, her hands on the shoulders of a little girl with a finger crooked over her lip as she watched us stream by.

That was more than thirty years ago, but it is still hard to shake the revival feeling. It would be a relief to become my father, slipping out of myself into visions of heaven, my face and hands raised to the sky. But I know believing in those days would mean pitting myself against others in the worst sense, as if I were climbing a shaft of light shining down from the mountain and they were sinking into the river, down into the green grave beneath the shadow of the Kootenai.

THREE

Purple Gold

The old blue Ford grumbles up the gravel switchbacks, rattling over washboard ruts in the road. My father drives with one hand, jimmying the stick shift with the other as my mother sits by his side, her hands folded in her lap, gazing over the dusty dashboard into the predawn dark. My sister's head bounces on my shoulder as I lean against the passenger door, my head cradled against the seatbelt. The ruts have banished all hope of sleep, so I stare out the bug-splattered windshield at the alder branches thumping against the hood. As we round a corner and break into a clearcut the trees fall away and the truck bumps along the edge of a steep drop-off. The sky opens up. Dark ridges and ravines roll out to the west, where a river runs between the mountains. A crescent moon hangs above the horizon, stars fading as day breaks. Then we're back in the trees, skidding up another switchback toward the top of the clearcut. The brakes groan as my father brings the truck to rest at the edge of the forest. The slope drops into thick brush, the open hillside riddled with stumps of old fir and larch. We've arrived at the huckleberry patch.

I leap from the cab to stretch my legs. It is late July, but a cold breeze sweeps down the mountain before sunrise. My sister and I cinch down our hoodies, shivering. We're dressed in our oldest clothes, our jeans blotched by purple stains where we've mashed berries against our knees. I dig around in the pickup bed for a rag that I'll use as a belt, running the cloth under the pail handle and knotting the ends like a drawstring around my waist. My father has packed several five-gallon buckets, a few smaller pails, and a couple of large coolers to hold the day's harvest. Though we face a long day of work, I tingle with anticipation the way a marathoner might at the starting line. I think of the money I'll make when we take the berries to market, as much as two hundred dollars from today alone if I really buckle down. It's the only way I'll get new clothes for school, and I'll be in eighth grade this year, so I'm determined to look my best. As I tie the pail to my waist, I picture the stonewashed Levi's and Bugle Boy shirts I want to buy.

Fog cloaks the valley as the sun lights up the high country. I shade my eyes and gaze at the peaks to the north, bouncing on my toes to keep warm. No matter how much I dread waking before dawn, I come alive at sunrise, my chest swelling with the widening sky. The huckleberry patch is a secret we keep from everyone but family and the closest friends, and I feel that way about the view. My Montana. The Last Best Place. Some of my friends are mowing lawns for the summer, and I know I'm lucky to be here instead, where I can see as far as Canada.

When my mother and sister have chosen their pails and my father slams the tailgate shut with his own buckets bobbing from his belt, we split up for the day. I slip across the mountain in solitude, losing myself among the alder. For another child it would be drudgery, but I love being alone in the forest. Flesh and spirit merge as I move through the bushes in silence. A bull moose steps into a distant clearing, turns his enormous rack of antlers toward me, and lopes hundreds of yards up the steep slope, disappearing into the fir and spruce. A chipmunk scrabbles up a stump to watch me work, twitching its tail as I bend to my task. The trick is to fall into a partial trance, like a pianist who finds the middle space between distraction and overexertion. Part of me focuses on the berries, both hands gently stripping the bush, eyes roaming for the next patch as a bird trills, *chick-a-dee-dee-dee-dee.* The rest of me drifts through dreams, the curve of a purple berry conjuring thoughts of the football coach's daughter, which makes me think of the two-a-day practices starting in August and the plastic taste of water from the Rubbermaid cooler, so different from the spring water we drink at home.

Then I think of the spring in the woods behind our house, bubbling out of the ground in an endless supply. I'm lost in that thought for a while, meditating on the burbling mystery of water, the way it murmurs and glitters in the sun. One of my teachers has a way of saying water as *werder* which I like for its softness, though words can never encompass the dancing, shape-changing thing. All the while the taut flesh of huckleberries roll through my fingers into the bucket, my daydreams playing over the bushes and trees.

Huckleberries are a staple for bears, so I stiffen with alarm when I hear a stick snap nearby. One of my uncles often tells the story of being treed by a sow with cubs one fall while scouting elk for the upcoming hunting season. The snort in the bushes startled him, and when the sow stood on her hind legs—a cinnamon brown bear over seven feet tall—he scarcely had time to leap into a small fir tree before she charged, ripping up after him and slashing at his boots. The treetop bent under their weight as he kicked desperately at her snarling snout, trying to stay clear of her claws. One of his kicks struck home, and the sow fell from the tree, grunting as she hit the ground. For over an hour she lay at the base of the fir, gnashing her teeth whenever he moved, until she finally gathered her cubs and cleared out.

While many pickers carry handguns or pepper spray, my parents believe antagonizing a bear will only worsen the danger. My mother feels she could speak soothingly to a bear if it comes to that, and it is fortunate she's never had to test this theory. When I was very young she read to me from *Blueberries for Sal* about a mother and child who go to the woods to gather berries. Just over the hill a sow and its cub are browsing in a berry patch. Young Sal and the cub wander away from their mothers to eat their fill. When they try to find their way back, they each mistakenly follow the sound of the wrong mother, Sal stumbling upon the sow and the cub surprising Sal's mother. All ends well, as one expects in a children's book, and there is some of this innocent faith in my parents' belief that the forest is not a truly dangerous place.

But there are risks as we inch across the slope for ten hours a day, with our hands occupied and several pounds dangling from our waists. Falling is inevitable, and my first thought is to keep from spilling my bucket at all costs. If I take a false step, I lift the pail with one arm and turn the opposite shoulder into the fall, bruising my shoulders on rocks and gashing my back against jagged logs. But living with risks is essential to any meaningful creativity, and this is the logic behind my parents' refusal to carry a gun into the berry patch. They believe we should carry our wits with us instead.

By noon the sun is hot overhead, and the musk of the forest duff rises from the ground as I make my way back to the truck for lunch, cinching a lid over my pail for safekeeping. My mother has baked my favorite Czech rolls stuffed with ground elk, sauerkraut, and cheese. We munch on garden carrots and molasses gingersnaps before tying empty buckets to our waists and heading out again until evening.

I know I need to carry as many gallons off the hill as I can, so I can buy the latest Air Jordan shoes for basketball season, but I also find pleasure in the gathering, watching the harvest swell in my pail. As I caress the bushes with my thumb and forefinger, pouring each handful into the bucket, the berries drum on the bottom like a heavy rain. Soon the base of the pail disappears, the purple mound rising as I straighten and bend and coax the berries into my hands, dreaming all the while.

As the day winds down I carry my bucket back to the truck, my feet aching from traversing the slope. As we wait for my father, I hunt for a stick the size of a baseball bat and wander the road at the edge of the clearing where light lingers longest, tossing up stones and whacking them as far as I can against the pale yellow sky, watching them arc over the horizon. After nightfall my father surfaces from the dark, and I hold a flashlight as he spreads newspaper in the bottom of our twenty-gallon cooler, pouring the glistening berries in layers, each bucketful cushioned by a fresh sheet of paper.

The next day we'll lift a layer at a time onto the dining table to clean the dark mounds in handfuls, tossing the leaves and stems into one bowl and the fruit into another. Then we'll pass our goods to the end of the table, where my father fills the freezer bags with a quart-sized measuring cup. It takes two or three hours to clean a day's picking, so we spin LPs on an old turntable, working to "Monday, Monday" and "Tangled Up in Blue." For days afterward my fingers carry the purple stain like a reminder of the wild woods.

Huckleberries became known as purple gold during the Great Depression, when miners built sluice boxes to clean the berries, rolling them down a chute to filter debris. Some berry camps set up makeshift canneries in the woods, shipping the jars off to Spokane and Missoula. Black workers migrated through from Seattle, weaving summer huts of bear grass and willow, and the Kootenai tribe set up tipi camps from Libby to Bonners Ferry. But few fortunes were made in this business. It was mostly a fall-back plan for "folks in hard straits," as a forest ranger wrote in 1933.

We sometimes stumbled onto the broken branches and mashed berries left by pickers who spread a sheet of canvas on the ground and beat the bushes with a cloth racket, gathering the berries in a shower of leaves and twigs. The beaters, as we called them, could get as many as fifty gallons per day, but even on our best outings my sister and I were lucky to get five gallons apiece while my mother and father might edge closer to ten. This was a sacrifice my parents were willing to make and one I honor now, because I understand they cared about more than the money we made. They wanted us to take care in the woods, to leave the mountain as we found it.

By the time my sister and I were learning the trade, my parents filled orders with a local chocolate maker, then froze the rest of the crop in gallon-sized bags to take on the road. The berries pulped by the beaters turned to a solid block of ice in the freezer, but because we picked and cleaned our huckleberries by hand, each one froze individually. This allowed my father to pull a frozen Ziploc bag from his cooler and shake out an exact cup, a stunt that wowed gourmet chefs in Missoula and Bozeman, who sometimes paid us as much as fifty dollars per gallon. Other buyers ran gift shops, where huckleberry syrups and jams and pancake mixes were the most prized of Montana souvenirs, the very taste of how life used to be.

———————

Every huckleberry picker has a bonanza story. Ours came one August after a mild spring, when rain fed the mountainside through July. My parents knew of a clearcut in the Bull River Valley approaching its peak yield, just on the verge of being taken over by alder and lodgepole pines. The road to the berry patch was gated for grizzly habitat, so chances of competing with other pickers were slim.

It was at least an hour's drive to the gate, then a bit of a hike to the patch, so we piled into the pickup before sunrise. My sister slept on my shoulder as I dozed against the shoulder strap, the tires humming over the highway. The cab smelled of clean cotton and sawdust, and the seat vibrated with the feeling of hurtling toward the day's work.

My father took a turn from the main highway onto a dirt road. The truck shimmied on the ruts as it climbed the switchbacks. Alder branches thumped against the side mirrors. Then there was a green gate across the road, the frame bent at the hinges where someone had tried to ram it off the post. The mountain was still in shadow as we slid from the cab, mosquitoes whining about our heads as we gathered our gear. My father packed a garden cart with our buckets and coolers, slipping the handle over his chest and walking the cart up the road like a rickshaw.

We climbed for what felt like an hour before the tree canopy opened at the edge of the clearcut, where a steep dirt bank angled up to the duff. My father said, "Look." We followed his eyes, and we could see the berries from the road, a sea of bushes heavy with fruit. Adrenaline kicked in then, and we rushed to gather our buckets, scrambling up the embankment and out into the brush and the stumps.

Filling a bucket was usually hard work, but it felt effortless that day because the berries were the size of nickels and dimes, firm and ready to fall from the stem with a gentle touch. For hours I stroked the bushes free of berries in shades of frosty blue, red, and black, all nearly bursting from their skins. My knees ached from kneeling too long, my lower back cramping from the weight of the pail. Each berry bled a little where it left the stem, my hands darkening with each blot, staining my face when I wiped away the sweat.

Dusk fell, and a full moon rose. My father was the last to quit, picking by moonlight until he'd topped off every bucket and cooler the cart could hold. There were hundreds of gallons of berries on the mountain, bliss for the grizzlies and for us. As a family we'd gathered over thirty gallons, less than a single beater could get, but still the finest harvest we'd ever known. As my father eased the cart down the mountain, taking care not to lose his footing on the steep pitch of the switchbacks, I wandered ahead, trailing my hands over the alder leaves on the roadside and gazing up at the moon, trying to identify trees by their profiles against the night sky. The wings of the spruce. Ramrod trunks of the tamaracks. Great sweeping boughs of the fir. My mother and sister held hands, skipping down the pitted road, where gravel gleamed between the shadows. Soon we reached the gate, the truck looming out of the dark. The cart creaking as my father brought it to rest. Buckets and coolers scraping over the truck bed. Then the slam of the tailgate and the warm shoulder-to-shoulder closeness with my sister in the cab.

I did not sleep on the drive home. I was ringing like a struck pipe with a feeling of triumph. This memory I want to keep safe, bearing witness to a moment when I liked who I was and who we were together at the end of a sweet day of labor.

FOUR

The Power Team

The arena was packed. I crouched in the middle of the crowd, throwing ghost punches at Wheeler, who stood over six feet and weighed at least two hundred pounds. Wheeler was dark and handsome, enormous for a high school freshman. We were church friends, regulars in the youth group, which was why we'd come to Dahlberg Arena in Missoula, home of the Montana Grizzlies. We'd been waiting for this show for weeks after the church took a special offering one Sunday to raise money for our tickets.

Wheeler ducked under my left jab and pretended to rock me with a knockout uppercut. I let my hands go slack, as if I'd been hurt, and staggered back against Ken, our youth leader, a short, stocky man with shoulder-length hair.

"Take it easy, guys," Ken said, catching my shoulders and shoving me back upright. Then the lights cut out. For a moment we were blinded, and silence fell over the crowd. We heard a ghostly wail from the speakers hanging over the basketball court, like a rushing wind, which I recognized as the beginning of a song by Idle Cure. I tensed in anticipation of the singer's opening shout: "Break away!" Smoke bathed in purple light rose from the floor as the guitars kicked in, and we began clapping and cheering, my pulse racing to the drumbeat as I sang along with the refrain, "Leave behind the old life." The smoke turned golden, as if lit by a furnace, and then we saw them running out onto the floor like warriors through a fallen city, their giant arms upraised. It was John Jacobs and the Power Team, a group of bodybuilders and evangelists who toured the country performing feats of strength—smashing stacks of flaming bricks with their foreheads and bench-pressing hundreds of pounds while lying on a bed of nails—working themselves and the crowd into hysterics before telling their testimonies about how they left gang violence to follow Christ, how they overcame drug addiction or sexual promiscuity through God's help: stories that left teens weeping and ready to answer the altar call at the end of the show, when all the adrenaline had been spent and nothing seemed more soothing than prayer.

That night I watched with amazement as a man took a one-inch steel bar in his hands and bent it into a pretzel, veins bulging along his biceps. Another took a run at a row of eight ice blocks, each a foot thick and about four feet tall, lowering his shoulder and shattering each of them, shards exploding around his head. John Jacobs saved the most dramatic events for himself, locking two sets of metal handcuffs to his wrists to illustrate the bondage of sin, then stretching the links against his enormous chest—fists clenched—dropping his hands as if discouraged and asking us to help him find the strength, straining once more to snap the cuffs and bowing his head as he failed, asking us to scream louder, then straightening a third time with his head back and teeth bared, elbows shaking as he lifted his chest, gave a shout, and snapped the chains in two.

Just before the altar call, Jacobs carried a stack of thirty baseball bats to center stage, accompanied by Carman's hit song, "The Champion," which dramatized the death and resurrection of Christ as an epic boxing match between Jesus and Satan. Jacobs began snapping the bats one by one over his leg, stepping forward in a lunge and bracing the bat against his upper thigh, gripping the base in one hand and the barrel in the other, pressing his bulk downward until the handle splintered. He destroyed another bat, then another, the pile of ruined wood rising at his side until he was down to one Louisville Slugger at the point in the song when Satan realized his knockout punch had not really killed Christ, that the Son of God was coming back to life, and as Carman built toward the climax, his voice shaking with passion, Jacobs' arms began trembling as if he could not break the last one, the crowd nearly delirious as Carman sang "He has won" and Jacobs crushed the bat, lifting the broken pieces above his head in the shape of a cross and circling the stage as Carman drew out the chorus, "He's alive forevermore, he has risen, he is Lord."

Young people poured from the bleachers to kneel on the wrestling mats with Jacobs and the other hulking men they'd spread over the basketball court, and all of the lowered voices in the stadium merged in a gentle thunder. Wheeler and I sat with our heads bowed, Ken standing at our side, his arms raised, cheeks streaked with tears. After a spell we gathered the rest of the youth group and boarded the church bus for home. It was a quiet ride, Ken squinting into the night, watchful for deer as we wound through the Clark Fork Valley. When he grew sleepy, Ken slid in a cassette by Petra, which meant "rock" in Greek. Petra sounded a little like Led Zeppelin with their shrill vocals and *wa-wa* riffs, but this was a praise album with tunes more suitable for a Sunday service, and we sang along in the dark. I sat alone, my knees propped against the seat in front of me as I watched the shadowy landscape speed past, lifting my voice with the others to the chorus of "Take Me In" and "Salvation Belongs to Our God."

I'd attended revival services my whole life, but even though I'd been baptized and wanted to believe I was saved, part of me was always holding back, unable to join in. At one evening service, desperate for a breakthrough, I bent at the altar, asking the minister to pray with me for a spiritual gift. He was a big man with thick black hair and a powerful voice, and I felt sure he could lift me to higher ground. I wanted the assurance I could see in my parents, the kind of trancelike surrender it seemed everyone but me could achieve, and so I knelt with my eyes squeezed shut, listening to the minister's whispered prayer and waiting for lightning to strike my heart. Nothing happened. My chest was sealed shut. The minister grew weary of my silence and seized both of my wrists, trying to raise my arms. "Can't you praise the Lord?" he hissed. I struggled against him, mortified, and he let me go in disgust.

Tonight felt different. There was no pressure to shout or dance or wave my hands, uttering prophecies. The Power Team simplified faith to strength and endurance. I could identify with the way Jacobs strained against his handcuffs as if wrestling with his own body. This was a message I could live out, a way of imagining pain as redemption. As Ken hit the homestretch to Troy through the Bull River Valley, the praise tape wound down and the bus fell silent. I felt the curtain of sleep falling as my pulse slowed. I settled against the seat, meditating on a new beginning. Here was a way to live without pretense, I thought, a muscular faith to seal my place among the believers. No fanfare, no miraculous gifts, just the daily ritual of iron and sweat, the gradual perfection of my flesh.

Before I went to bed that night, I pinned a Power Team poster to my wall. The row of somber men gazed down at me, their bulging arms crossed over their naked chests, reminding me where my allegiance lay. The next day I coaxed my father into buying a telescoping pull-up bar, which we wedged into the doorjamb in the laundry room. Every morning before school I struggled through a circuit of pull-ups and sit-ups and push-ups, hoping to save enough to purchase my own set of dumbbells. I was nowhere near the size of the men on my wall, but I looked to them daily for proof I could grow in body and soul.

This was more than vanity, more than bodybuilding for show. I'd been raised to think of faith in masculine terms, as a holy struggle. For years I was haunted by the Armageddon films I'd seen in Bible studies, cars abandoned on the highway after the rapture, Soviet soldiers marching into American towns and breaking down doors to slaughter families in cold blood when they refused to renounce their beliefs. My parents bought Frank Peretti's Christian thrillers *This Present Darkness* and *Piercing the Darkness* and I read with amazement about angels and devils battling unseen in the air around us. One demon was described as a vulture sitting atop a woman's head, its talons sunk deep into her brain as she unknowingly did its bidding. Even though I didn't believe the world really worked that way, it was a difficult image to shake, and I sometimes found myself watching my teachers, imagining birds of prey clutching their skulls. Then again, how would I know if my own brain were seized by a demon? Even in everyday life the stakes seemed high.

My girlfriend, Tess, grew tired of all the God talk. She was a willowy blond with curly hair cut just above her shoulders, a thin girl who wore loose cream-colored sweaters and tight acid-washed jeans. We were classmates in eighth grade, making eyes at one another for weeks before I mustered the nerve at the spring picnic to ask her out, by which I meant did she want to go steady. She did. It was a sunny June day, and we wandered away from the campground where our teachers shoved hot dogs around on the grill, down a trail winding away from the parking lot into the forest along the Yaak River. In summer the water turned clear as the river dropped away from the banks, coursing quietly over its rocky bed, but it was spring and snow was melting in the mountains, sliding into the valley for miles upstream. The river was muddy and strong, the roar of the water cutting us off from the group as we walked along the shore. Now and then we heard a rumble as the current caught a boulder and rolled it downstream.

The rushing water gave me courage, and I took her hand in mine, a soft thrill warming my belly. We walked like that for a few moments, eyes cast down bashfully, and then Tess suddenly pressed our clasped hands to her chest. The pressure of her breast gave me vertigo. A spike of adrenaline shot up my neck. Just moments before, I'd been searching for the right words, uncertain of her answer, and we had rocketed forward to this. My pulse thudded in my ears, and I was a little relieved when we heard one of the teachers shouting over the river, calling us back to the bus. We sat together on the ride home, and this time Tess took my hand. Our classmates teased us, as they did all new lovebirds, but they soon lost interest and we drifted into a dreamy silence as the ruckus of the others fell away. Tess lifted my hand to her lap, worming the fingers of her free hand into the knot we had made. We rode like that all the way back to school, my face flushed from the warmth of her legs and the vigor of her hands gripping mine like a vise.

It became a familiar feeling with Tess, the thrill of touch spiked with alarm and the cold surge of dread that followed. I knew it seemed unnatural to her that I sometimes drew back, afraid, while other boys my age had their hands up their girlfriends' shirts during study hall. When we were apart my thoughts ran wild, but when we were together my chest tightened defensively, the way it had when the minister gripped my wrists. Whenever Tess nudged me too far, nibbling on my ear or slipping her tongue into my mouth as we kissed, it was the surprise that spooked me, the feeling that she took more than I was ready to give. Ken sometimes spoke in youth group about how promiscuous he'd been in high school, which he believed was the reason his first marriage failed. "The body is a temple," he said, "and you lose something special when you desecrate it." Ken was remarried, and he brought his wife, Jill, to one of our meetings to encourage the girls to stay strong. Jill was a brunette with big hair and slender hips and full, pouty lips, and it seemed cruel to have to listen to her talk about sex. "Hold a penny between your knees if you have to," she joked to the girls. "And you guys, keep it sweet. Sometimes a girl will do anything for acceptance, but if you treat her with respect she'll love you so much more." I was doing my best, but this required a crystalline view of Tess, which shattered every time we met.

Tess believed in God, but she didn't think it was anybody's business whether she was *saved* or not, as she said with scorn when I asked her if she wanted to come to youth group. "I don't have to go to church to be a Christian," she said. "Jesus didn't go to youth group, did he?"

Maybe not, I said, but even if you don't have to show up on Sunday to believe in God, if you really believe, you'll want to go.

"And if you really believe," Tess snapped, "you'll know what's between me and God is none of your business." Her allure trumped any misgivings I might have had about our differences, which I explained away as a test of my faith. It would take many years to recognize that the bad girl's appeal sometimes lies less in her minxy air than in her potential to be redeemed, and though I could not have expressed this then, I surely stuck with Tess because the conquest would not be complete until I'd won her both heart and soul.

Ken was challenging us to take a stand in high school, to let people know who we were and what we believed. Jill organized a youth group meeting every Wednesday during the lunch hour, so we could keep each other going throughout the week. Tess refused to go and couldn't believe I'd choose a prayer group over time with her, so the tension between us steadily rose. Things did not improve when Wheeler and I bought T-shirts with Christian logos adapted from popular brands, Gold's Gym recast as God's Gym, and Reebok changed to Reeborn. "That's so dumb," Tess said, when she saw my newest shirt with a red Lord's Gym logo above an image of Christ doing a push-up beneath a heavy cross. I was a little self-conscious about the back of the shirt, too, which bore a bloody hand pierced by a nail and the words, HIS PAIN YOUR GAIN. But I was still riding the wave of the Power Team, and I welcomed a little hostility as proof of my faith. "If people get in your face," Ken said, "you know you've got their attention." Tess thought there was a difference between being persecuted and actively seeking out abuse, and I could see her point.

I raised a similar issue at our weekly lunch meeting when Wheeler said he didn't mind being known as a "Jesus Freak." If people think you're a freak, I said, why should they listen to what you have to say? Don't you need a little cred if you expect them to take you seriously? Ken retorted that if you cared about what other people thought, then you weren't really hardcore committed to God. What good is being hardcore, I said, if it makes you so ridiculous people won't even have a conversation with you? Ken was familiar with these arguments. "God chose the foolish things of the world to shame the wise," he said. "And God chose the weak things of the world to shame the strong."

Ken liked getting the last word and usually cut off debate by asking us to join hands and bow our heads, when we were encouraged to offer up prayer requests. This was the part of youth group that felt real, when we all closed our eyes and fell silent, each voice speaking softly in turn, Jill squeezing my hand with her tiny fingers, Wheeler anchoring me on the other side. There could be no conflict here, no doubts nibbling at my thoughts, just the balm of words, the gentle babble of sound. I lost track of the prayer and drifted into daydreams, my inner space suddenly vast, as if I were hurtling out of orbit, past the moon, out toward Jupiter and Saturn's hypnotic rings. After a time I heard Ken's voice from a great distance, "And all God's people said . . ." Then I was back in my body, rumbling "amen" with the others, squinting in the afternoon light as I remembered Tess was sulking somewhere outside this circle.

At one of the meetings I asked the group to pray for Tess. Her mother and stepfather were on the outs, waking Tess late at night with their screaming. It felt harmless at the time to offer this up, out of concern and what I felt was love, but Tess did not take it that way when someone from the group let her know she'd been on our list. I was closing my locker between classes, books in one hand, when she shoved me from behind. My head slammed against the metal door, my books falling to the floor.

"What's this about you asking people to *pray* for me?" Tess yelled. "You can go to hell if you think you're so superior. I *trusted* you." She waited for a moment with her hands on her hips, eyes red from crying. When I could find no words, she threw down her hands and said, "Forget it. You're so clueless. Get out of my life!"

Blood roared in my ears as I gathered my things, and I stormed into the next class, the lump on my head throbbing. I slumped in the wooden desk, arms crossed, staring at a photo of a human pyramid on the cover of the Geometry textbook. Mr. Bulinski paced at the front of the room, a short, portly man with a handlebar mustache and curly black hair rising like smoke from his thinning pate. He had grown up in Chicago and posted Cubs trivia on the board each day, sometimes regaling us with memories of playing bass in a hippie band or writing his proofs in graduate school with colored pencils. He rode a Harley to school and wore jeans and Chuck Taylor high-tops, and we usually hung on his every word. If we did not, if we began talking among ourselves, he walked into the supply closet, shut the door, and screamed, a stunt that never failed to snap us back on task.

But nothing could reach me that afternoon. Or the next day. For a week I swung between cursing myself for betraying Tess and wallowing in the sweet-sour ache of her absence, longing for the peach-scented shampoo in her hair, the soft burn of desire when I walked with her hand in mine. She ignored me in the hall, walking away each time I tried to apologize, and finally I gave up. The end of the quarter came and went, my thoughts bouncing like tumbleweeds through the final tests.

My father was none too pleased by my report card. "You're better than this," he said. "Almost all Bs? You've got to buckle down." There was a man he wanted me to meet who might be able to help. Sid was one of our neighbors, a former bodybuilder who retired to Montana after selling his health club in San Francisco. While surveying his property boundary, my father learned that Sid had an attic packed with vintage exercise gear, a full rack of steel dumbbells, a bench press and an incline press, two cable machines, even a weight stack with a padded bar for leg curls. Sid offered us free run of his upstairs gym, and my father thought this might help get my head on straight, so I began dropping by after school, determined to purge Tess from my mind and start the next quarter with more focus. Finally I had a chance to pump some real iron. I felt sure that once my arms and chest thickened out, my faith would grow, too.

———————

Every afternoon I rode the bus to Sid's driveway, a long gravel path framed by a cattle guard. A wooden sign leaned among the weeds with the name Galena Ranch burned into the boards. The fields where the previous owner grazed cattle, some five or six acres, had turned mostly to knapweed and alfalfa except for one low-lying flat Sid had converted to a pond. Sid's main hobby, whenever he wasn't working out, was paddling over the pond, dumping clay into holes dug by a muskrat he hunted daily, drifting in his little rowboat with a shotgun cradled between his knees. He kept at it until the pond froze over, hunched on his seat in a pair of insulated coveralls.

Sid was a barrel-chested man, about six feet tall, with fleshy jowls and a staccato laugh. He nearly died of fever as a child, running a temperature for over a week, and he'd been bald ever since. "No armpit hair, nuthin," he said, grinning. Without so much as eyebrows it was hard to tell how old he was, though I guessed early sixties, gauging the age of his wife, Betty, by the deep creases lining her face. They made a copy of the house key so I could let myself in if they were out. But most days I found Sid crouched in his dingy on the pond and Betty bent over her crossword at the kitchen table, scarcely looking up after I banged through the back door and climbed the steep staircase to the attic, pulling myself up along the railing. I grew to like the scent of mothballs and rubbing alcohol upstairs as I changed into my workout gear. The little gym became a second home.

The attic had been remodeled with a thin maroon carpet and pine paneling, along the ceiling, which was scarcely high enough to clear the top of the cable machines. Inside the door at the top of the stairs stood an inclined sit-up mat, an empty bench for seated curls, and a wooden bookcase where I kept my workout charts. The dumbbell rack sat against the far wall, the weights scuffed and faded from frequent use. The south end of the attic opened through a sliding glass door to a tiny sunroom where the leg curl machine sat next to a rocking chair that looked out over the fields, the driveway, and the pond, where I could see Sid in his boat, tiny in the distance.

When I first talked to Sid about using his gym, he showed me some of his old bodybuilding photos. His body glistened with oil, legs chiseled like wood grain, veins knotting his arms. "In this one, I'm already going to pieces," he said, pointing to a shot where he wore a wavy wig that made him look like Frank Sinatra, his perfect teeth gleaming as he posed from the side, hands locked together and one arm curled in profile. Sid laughed and rubbed his belly. "Now I'm just a fat old man. But believe it or not I still have some abs under all this blubber."

Sid coached me through the first week, guiding my hands on the bench press bar, demonstrating how to suck in a deep breath before pushing up, exhaling quickly and drawing in more air before each repetition. He showed me how to adjust the pulleys on the crossover cable machine, how to keep my arms straight to work my back muscles. "Don't worry about the weight," he said. "If you want to get cut, you've got to focus on form." He reached across his body with one arm, slapping his back under his armpit. "You've got to concentrate. If you don't feel the burn in the right spot, you're wasting your time."

After that he left me to myself, and I settled into the routine, grinding through the sit-ups, then the squats and lunges, wrapping up with the chest, back, and arms. It was meditative, like prayer, and I grew addicted to the pain, the feeling of burning out as Sid put it, when I would strain for one last bicep curl and let the weight slowly back down, arms shrieking with acid. I began to understand how monks could fast for days, how self-inflicted weakness became a kind of strength. I could lose myself in the fifteen repetitions of a set of lunges, careful with my balance as I stepped forward, lowering one knee nearly to the ground, focusing on my quads as I straightened and took another step, the pain rising until my legs were shaking and all else seared away except for the next lunge and the last coals of strength as I strained to finish the set. I moved from one routine to another in silence broken only by the creaking floor, the puff of each breath, and the clang of the weights in the rack. Tess faded from my thoughts as I grappled with my body the way John Jacobs had when he described his struggle with sin, swelling his chest against the double set of handcuffs locked to his wrists and groaning until he broke the chains. Each afternoon I called my mother to pick me up. "How was your day?" she'd ask as I slouched in the seat, my strength so spent I could scarcely reply.

One cloudy afternoon, in the pale winter light trickling into the attic through the sunroom, I began exploring the bookcase. I'd been so absorbed by the weight routine that I'd scarcely given it a glance, sliding my chart onto a lower shelf at the end of the day. But as I was catching my breath between sets of seated curls, I scanned the titles at eye level, recognizing *Walden* and *The Scarlet Letter* among the exercise books, Boy Scout manuals, and finance guides. Another title caught my eye, printed in a big block-letter font: *Love Slave*. Silence grew thick in my ears as I hooked a finger over the spine, pulled it from the shelf, and studied the cover. A woman stood with a lash raised over her head, dressed in nothing but a leather vest and knee-high stiletto boots, the spike of one heel resting on the bare buttocks of another woman who knelt, hands bound behind her back, below the tail of the whip. Vertigo washed over me, the way it had with Tess when she pressed her breasts against me. I opened the book, fingers trembling, and found more drawings of the mistress and her slave, hands shackled above her head, wrists tied to her ankles, head and arms pinned in a wooden stockade.

I felt something drop within me, a cold sinking feeling mingled with fascination, and it was many minutes before I put the book back and stood, shaking, my legs stiff from sitting so long. I walked out into the sunroom, looking down on the pond where Sid was stalking the shoreline in his fishing waders, shotgun cradled in the crook of his arm. Betty stirred downstairs, and I spun around, my heart racing, as if I'd been found out. Struggling to forget what I'd just seen, I rushed through a set of curls and started the bench press, groaning as I pushed each set to the maximum, my arms shuddering as I dropped the bar in the rack with a sigh. At the end of the routine I did an extra set of squats as if in penance, burning out so thoroughly my knees nearly buckled as I descended the stairs.

The images haunted my thoughts the next day, drifting over my line of sight the way my yearning for Tess had, and I wondered if Sid's book might be a demonic force clutching at my mind. As Mr. Bulinski paced in Geometry class, working out proofs on his overhead transparencies, my thoughts wandered to a girl in the front row, and then I saw the ropes and chains and the mistress's whip upraised, and I shook myself as if from sleep, imagining a hawk above my head with its talons sinking through my skull. This was crazy—I knew it was crazy—but it seemed like my body was slipping out of control even as I sought to subdue it with the daily ritual. I was starting to lose the sense I had felt on the bus ride home after the Power Team show, when it seemed like I might really have a chance at saving my soul.

That afternoon I stepped off the bus at the Galena Ranch like it was any other day. Part of me longed to flee the cramped attic, but part of me ached to return. It was nearly Christmas, but the ground was still soft and muddy as I walked up the drive, waving to Sid in his boat on the pond. I slipped through the back door, said hello to Betty, and climbed the stairs. My face flushed as I changed, battling the urge to pull the book back off the shelf. I made it through one set of lunges before I caved, my vision blurring as I flipped through the pages, my pulse racing even as my belly weakened with guilt.

The cold flood of shame finally snuffed my desire, and I returned to the lunges, lifting one foot forward and lowering the opposite knee to the ground, straightening and repeating on the other side. The rhythm soothed me, and so did the fire building in my thighs. Between sets I fought to keep my thoughts from wandering back to the shelf, and then I strained away at the next routine, slipping a pin into the weight stack, gripping the wide-angled handles of the overhead bar as I settled onto my knees, hauling the bar down ten, twelve, fifteen times until it just grazed the back of my neck, focusing on the burn along my back as my arms weakened and shook. There was a purity in exhaustion, a cleansing always within reach. It made me feel that whatever I'd done to Tess or whatever we'd done together was somehow absolved, that even if I returned to Sid's book, even if I saw things there that would linger in my thoughts for days, I could work up a sweat and wash it all away.

Every school day, straight on into spring, I stopped at the Galena Ranch, a little stronger each day, my chest and arms thickening, my legs a little firmer beneath me every morning until I tore them down in Sid's attic and wobbled home. I had no energy left for anything but dinner and homework and bed. Youth group with Wheeler and Ken over the weekend. Prayer lunch at midweek. And if I woke feverish from dreams of shadows and red light, cracking lashes and shrieks of what could be pain or ecstasy, there was always the bench press at the end of the day, the agony of a hundred sit-ups, and the sweet flood of relief as I fell back against the mat.

As I lay there panting one day, gazing at the panels of knotty pine in the ceiling, I made a pact with myself. No dating, no parties, no distractions. After blowing my first-quarter tests, I wouldn't finish at the top of the class, but I'd get as close as possible. Then I'd go to college, get a job, buy a house, and when I really had my ducks in a row, I'd see about getting married. Years later I would think of this day when I heard someone say that announcing your plans is a good way to make God laugh. But it seemed simple then. I peeled myself off the mat and turned my back to the bookcase. Lifting a barbell to my waist, then heaving it to my chest, over my head, and down onto my shoulders, I began counting out squats. I had only planned to do twenty, but then I thought of John Jacobs breaking thirty bats over his leg, and I felt a sudden surge of purpose. As I lowered myself for the last repetition, thighs trembling, my belly nearly cramping with fatigue, it took everything I had to stand, and in the final moment of pain, just before my knees locked and blood rushed back into my legs, there was nothing in my head at all but a white, empty light.

FIVE

The Wide World

On summer days when I was a small child, after the sun had risen high enough to burn the dew from the grass, my mother spread a quilt beneath a plum tree and took my sister and me out to read. It was a tattered quilt cobbled from patches of old clothes my mother had stitched together by hand, and it was soft and cool to the touch. She spread it on the grass behind the house, in partial shade, so she could lie in the sun while my sister and I rested in the shadows, propped on our elbows and cradling our chins in our hands, awash with the smells of clover and cotton and sunscreen.

Then my mother read to us from *The Wind in the Willows*. Rat and Mole and Toad traveled the countryside, picnicking on riverbanks, tooling around in rowboats, and dodging scares from the Wild Wood, where Badger lived, and beyond which lay the Wide World. It was a rapturous dream, that story, and we sometimes had lunch immediately afterward, eating toast dripping with butter in honor of Toad, my mother once going so far as to make a sandwich of cold elk tongue, which I would never have stomached if it hadn't featured so prominently in a supper Mole and Rat and Badger enjoyed after evicting a pack of wild weasels from Toad's home. My mother wept while reading the seventh chapter, when Mole and Rat happen upon the Piper at the Gates of Dawn while searching for Portly, the baby otter who'd gone missing, and discover the little creature sleeping in the lap of the god Pan. "Why are you crying?" I asked. She smiled, wiped her eyes, and said, "Sometimes my cup just runs over."

I learned to read by age four, and I was surely trying to recapture the feeling of those magical mornings when I curled up with books as an older child. Draped in a corduroy quilt my mother crafted from a bear claw pattern, I disappeared for hours into *The Chronicles of Narnia* and Madeline L'Engle's *A Wrinkle in Time* and the adventures of James Herriot, the kindly veterinarian of Yorkshire, England, whose cheerful voice softened grisly accounts of rolling on a stable floor with his arm deep in a cow as he groped for a breached calf. Because my parents had banned television from our home, except for the World Series, I came to count books among my greatest pleasures, each one a threshold to a different world. By the time I began junior high, I was raiding my mother's stash of novels, struggling with Chaim Potok's *In the Beginning* but settling easily into *The Lord of the Rings* and *Where the Red Fern Grows*.

My bedroom occupied a corner of our daylight basement where the cement foundation emerged from the slope of the yard. One window opened at ground level, and three others looked out on the yard from the adjacent wall, where two chest freezers sat filled with venison and elk and gallon bags of huckleberries. The basement was unfinished, and the walls of my room were no more than two-by-four framing, which my mother covered with tie-dyed sheets. My door was a curtain cut from one of the sheets and draped over a rod wedged into the jamb. It was a precarious place to read, because my father often walked through the curtain without warning or rapped on the windows from outside when he saw me lounging with a book. He rarely read alone and looked askance at my doing so, particularly in the middle of the afternoon on a weekend, when he wanted help pulling weeds or pruning the raspberry canes.

If I knew my father was working outside, I often spread my quilt on the cement floor in the space between my bed and the freezers, where I could lie hidden from sight. Once, after peering through the windows to my room while I was hiding in the crevice, my father searched the entire house, hoping to enlist me in spreading a truckload of horse manure over the garden. Stymied, he finally barged through my door curtain in a rage that left him speechless when he found me on the floor in my pajama pants reading *White Fang*. Towering over me, his face nearly purple with anger, he gasped that I was to stop dillydallying, get dressed right now, and come make myself useful. In time I would learn the pleasure of working with my hands, but for many years, even after I started lifting weights and hustling through wind sprints at basketball practice and learning how to embrace pain as a sacrifice for my general sense of unworthiness, I preferred the freedom I found on the page to all else.

Though I chafed against my father's demands, he jostled me from my books often enough for me to think of reading as a form of sloth. And so, by the time I began high school and faced the question of what I would do with my life, I knew that, as much as I loved books, I could not possibly expect them to lead to success. The brush of cool cotton against my cheek, the deep green smell of the grass, the music of my mother's voice as she drew us into the saga of Rat and Mole and Toad—these were quaint memories. It was time to face the world armed with something more substantial than make-believe tales, time to take a stand for something real and decide what kind of man I would be.

If I could reach that boy now and reason with him, I would tell him to lighten up, let a little laughter in. I would say only a fool builds creeds from half-truths, that the surest way to prove false is to claim certainty. He would watch me warily, as he did all the others who offered similar counsel when he, the boy I once was, saw the world as a treacherous place riddled with snares. It's been said there are three kinds of people: some who learn by reading, others who learn by observation, and the rest who have to feel the hard knocks for themselves, like the prodigal who only comes around to the wisdom of his elders after wallowing in the muck. But where others might grieve over a youth squandered on cigarettes and cheap booze, I have the memory of bigotry to mourn. I craved simplicity then, the clear-eyed gaze of the true believer, and the higher I held the banner of faith, the more I railed against illicit sex and crimes against the unborn, the more my own words stung as they flew back at me.

―――――――

These were the early days of the culture wars, when the religious right mobilized and began building steam. After the Cold War collapsed, with Desert Storm come and gone, there was no common foe to rally Americans together, and we turned inward, against our neighbors and friends. Whether it was a sign of the times or just my awakening to public life as a young man, it seemed the Christians I knew were increasingly loath to let their light shine privately, shoving their way more and more from the sanctuary into the streets.

When I was a child listening to my mother read from Kenneth Grahame, my parents had a wide circle of friends, bearded anarchists, Mennonites, men who raised sheep and llamas, women who brought their wooden spinning wheels to our house and chatted with my mother for hours, working the treadles with their Birkenstock clogs and spinning yarn from baskets of white, fluffy wool as the wheels whirred and purred. On summer nights I remember bonfire parties where men picked their guitars as embers swirled against the starry sky. Labor rights loomed large during the timber and mining booms, and that was how my father positioned himself when he first ran for a county commissioner seat—as the ally of working people like my grandfather, who sometimes sat on lawn chairs with his union brothers outside the Libby lumber mill, where they might strike for a week or more, holding out for a better wage.

But after my father won his second campaign, the divide between public life and the pulpit shrank as the party platforms hardened along sharper lines. My father began weighing union rights against his social views, traveling with my mother to Washington, D.C., for the Rally for Life. After months of agonizing, my father switched parties, prompting the local newspaper to print a doctored photo of him in cross dress. I caught a lot of flak for being the commissioner's son, especially after his party shift, but I felt protective of my father's name in the town. As I struggled to behave like a man, it seemed there was no more room for the whimsies of the incorrigible Toad, and embracing the family stance toward the world made me steel myself as if for assault by an enemy.

In spite of all this, I was blessed with fine teachers who reached out to me, and one rose above them all. Mr. Faber was an old family friend with deep Montana roots, a lithe man with peppery hair and a deep voice projecting easily to the back of the room. I remember it as a gentle voice, soft but strong. He taught history and American government, coached the men's junior varsity basketball team, directed the drama productions, and oversaw a vocal ensemble, Reflections, which he accompanied on his keyboard at graduation. Decades earlier he had starred as a pitcher for the university team in Missoula, and I learned as much from him about how to be a whole person as I did about history, how to nurture the mind and the body and the musical ear.

There was just one thing about Mr. Faber that left me watchful. He was a liberal. He loved Jimmy Carter and Gandhi, and when he heard Bill Clinton claim he had never inhaled, Mr. Faber said, "Of course he did. And he loved it." As much affection as I felt for him, as rapt as I was every day in his class, I knew we stood on opposing sides of the culture wars. What I saw as signs of national decline, Mr. Faber cheered as civil liberty. He was my father's treasurer during the first campaign and supported him in the second, so Mr. Faber was one of many who felt betrayed by my father's decision to turn Republican in midstream.

No matter how much I imagined myself as a soldier of light, no matter how much I feigned civility, the sad fact was I did not understand how to separate conviction from judgment. Hate the sin, not the sinner, was the usual platitude, but deep down I knew this could never be true. I didn't want people to love me in spite of my beliefs. It was all or nothing: my faith was my life. It was a double standard to think it could be otherwise for Mr. Faber, sheer hubris to imagine I knew him better than he knew me.

The day Mr. Faber staged an abortion debate, when I ironed a blue pin-stripe shirt and cinched a red tie around my neck, girding myself to lead the pro-life side, is one of those memories that sharpens its emotional hue over the years. What seemed a golden triumph then I now see through the crimson veil of shame, in part for the stance I took, but more for how I took it, how desperately I wanted to win.

My mother sometimes called me a survivor of the holocaust on the unborn, since I was born after *Roe vs. Wade*. Her distrust of clinicians was so strong I was born at home, without a physician or midwife and only my father and the one witness noted on my birth certificate—Jesus Christ— to see me through. Near the end of my senior year, my parents adopted the first of four children, determined to show their commitment to the pro-life cause, and I joined the crusade. It seemed simple: life began at conception; any attempt to thwart it was murder. One day in an effort to get me to examine abortion from another perspective, Mr. Faber asked what

I might say to someone who felt condemning a woman to a life of poverty as a single mother, and also condemning the child to squalor, might be more grievous than abortion. Without hesitation, believing him to be posing his own stance hypothetically, I shot back, "I would tell him he was deceived." Mr. Faber smiled, which unnerved me. "I can accept that from you, Josh," he said.

The debate preparations became an all-consuming family affair, my mother and father and sister rehearsing the arguments with me over dinner each night. As I paged through the materials we'd gathered, I stumbled upon a cartoon I thought would stop everyone cold. It showed a cottage window in a German village, where a doctor addressed a frumpy woman with an enormous belly. "Your husband is a drunkard," the doctor said. "You, ma'am, have tuberculosis, and of your four children one has already died, one is blind, another deaf, and the third now also has TB. If I were you, I'd have an abortion, Mrs. Beethoven." The story was an urban legend, muddling the birth order (Beethoven was the eldest) and exaggerating disabilities and illnesses within the family, but it made my point, so I inquired no further. I was after the gotcha moment, the cheap thrill of abasing the other team, and it brought out a cynical side of me. It was a turning point like the moment a puppy has filled out and isn't as cute as he once was, when he's moved on from worrying the old tennis ball and is now curling his lip from his teeth, turning mean.

My mother and sister set themselves to cutting out chains of human profiles, dozens of stick people holding hands. My team and I were to tape these figures around the room before the debate to supplement a diagram distributed by the National Right to Life showing the number of casualties in each of the American wars compared to the number of abortions since 1973. Each figure represented ten thousand casualties. The Revolutionary War had a single stick figure for the roughly four thousand colonists killed. There was a long row of figures for the Civil War, slightly more for the two world wars combined, three figures for the Korean War, and six for nearly sixty thousand U.S. deaths in Vietnam. All told, this came to more than a million casualties. For the number of abortions since 1973, there were rows and rows of stick figures representing many millions, and the contrast was meant to be jarring. There were a lot of wars missing—countless battles with Native American nations, the Mexican-American

War, the Spanish-American War, and others, not to mention deaths by slavery—but it was a political illustration, not an attempt at real history. The point was not to muddy the waters.

On the day of the debate, my teammates and I tried taping the paper chains along the classroom walls and realized we could only circle the room once before the bell rang. When it came time to show the overhead slide listing the wars, I presented them in turn, sliding a manila folder down the transparency to hide the abortion statistics until the end. I kept the rest of the paper cutouts my mother and sister had labored over in a cardboard box at my elbow, and when I at last revealed the tally since *Roe vs. Wade*, I said, "Each one of these represents ten thousand children slaughtered since 1973." Panning the room with one arm to call attention to the chain taped above the windows and blackboard, I pulled the rest of the paper figures from the box with the other hand, dumping them on the floor at my feet in a long cascade.

A boy rose to his feet for the opposing side, his cheeks red with anger. "What is a life?" he asked the class, pointing at the pile I'd made. "How many trees did they kill to make all this? Why are we only talking about the life of the fetus and not the mother's life, or the father's life, or the life of the earth that has to feed all these people? What is a life?" A girl cried from the back of the class, "Isn't life all about doing the best with what you're given?" And for a few moments bedlam reigned before Mr. Faber calmed us and asked for our closing statements.

I don't remember if the class chose a winning side. I recall only the singularity of my purpose against all shadows of compromise. I burned with the clarity of my correctness, with a holy fire, the way I did at the end of a weightlifting circuit, when my body felt so weak it nearly fell away from my soul. Yet I wonder if what I felt then might also have been the seed of hate, the stiff shoot sprouting from intransigence and blind faith.

In the years to come, when I'd travel home from college for Christmas or summer vacation, a little wiser to the world, I sought out Mr. Faber, dropping by the high school to talk about St. Augustine's *Confessions* or to leave a copy of my Shakespeare paper, where I argued that the kings in the history plays could be read against Plato's idea of the just ruler. Every time I stopped to say hello, it was an unspoken apology for who I'd been just a few years earlier, a show of respect for a teacher who allowed me to find my own way. Mr. Faber asked questions, encouraging me to listen to how my answers sounded coming out of my own mouth. Because he encouraged me to search, I later understood that who I would become was perhaps not as crucial as who I was becoming and how attentive I was to each step along the way. But in high school this thought was like a morning star glimmering above a long stretch of railway, where I chugged ahead, stoking the white heat of my purpose and belching a sooty cloud over the sky.

While some of my classmates led the police on goose chases each weekend, sprinting into the timber whenever a patrol car might creep up to a party fire and nab the hapless ones passed out in the grass, I stayed home. There was a security in standing apart from the rest, like the feeling I got from climbing a crag high above the tree line, where I could look down at the rivers and valleys, gazing out toward the rim of the earth. It was a posture I later recognized in a college art class, the projector whirring as the professor clicked through the carousel, flashing a painting of a lone figure onto the screen, a man standing on a promontory above the sea and fog.

In most of my senior photographs I'm scowling, my jaw set in a firm line. This was the era of *Beavis and Butthead*, *The Simpsons*, and *Wayne's World*, when the grainy Atari games gave way to Nintendo—the false nirvana with the tinny, hypnotic music that could melt hours away until your thumbs grew raw from the controller pad. I was a sucker for movies and games when visiting friends, since I'd grown up without them at home, but I hated the way they made me feel after I surfaced from a marathon in front of the glowing screen, blinking and stupefied. I wanted more than anything to be taken seriously, which might have been why the profession I gravitated toward was among the most dour and humorless: I wanted to be a lawyer.

I'd never been in a courtroom, but I was drawn to the power of arguments, the way following a train of thought and persuading others of it seemed to yield either a win or a loss. It was in Mr. Faber's class, watching the film *Inherit the Wind*, based on the Scopes Monkey Trial—in which a teacher insisted on teaching evolution despite public outcry—that I first saw the high drama of the court, the cool authority of the judge, the tricky cross-examinations. Above all, I loved the impassioned pleas to the jury in the closing arguments. A lawyer, I thought, did not live in a dusky world. He made a case for the truth, and whether it prevailed or fell into disrepute rested squarely on his power to persuade. The painting of the man standing above the foggy sea, Friedrich's *Wanderer above the Mist*, was a fine illustration of the lawyer I wanted to become.

I began starching dress shirts each day before school, sometimes buttoning the top button, tie or no tie, just because I liked how a pressed shirt felt like an iron breastplate. And when I heard about the Close Up program, a weeklong tour of Washington, D.C., I knew I had to see the Supreme Court and the Senate and House chambers where the nation's laws were born.

———————

Washington, D.C. Marble everywhere, great white pillars and stone promenades, steam rising from the sewer grates, streets crammed with cars and wheezing buses, vendors pressing us with boiled peanuts and hot dogs and empanadas from their sidewalk carts. I'd raised money for months to pay for the trip, peddling boxed oranges and grapefruit, scooping popcorn at the high school concession stand during volleyball games, roaming the gymnasium during warm-ups to sell tickets for a 50/50 drawing at halftime, when a winner would take half the raffle pot. Now I was here with a hundred other students—several dozen from my hometown and other rural schools in Montana and a large group from New Mexico.

Each day began with a seminar or a meeting with one of our congressmen. I was wary of Max Baucus, a tall, tanned Democrat who seemed like too smooth a talker to be trusted. I'd heard rumors about Conrad Burns, an upstart Republican senator and former Marine who shocked his colleagues by wearing cowboy boots and dragging a spittoon onto the Senate floor. But when he showed up in a suit to meet with us, he seemed as slicked back as any other congressman. It was the first time I had seen people from my home state, both from ranching backgrounds, on a national stage. I could do this, too, I thought. Not in politics, but in the courts.

So when we met our sole U.S. representative, Pat Williams, whom I regarded as even more left wing than Baucus, I asked him to explain his voting record on abortion. My classmates hid their faces in their hands, weary of my diatribes, but it had become a rallying point for me, an argument I sought to perfect constantly. Representative Williams sensed the hostility in my question and paused a moment before answering, speaking with a softer voice, the way Mr. Faber posed questions in class. This is a difficult issue, he said. On the one hand you have a young woman who is terrified about what people are going to think of her, who might not have the support of the father, and who might lose her own life in childbirth. On the other hand, there is the unborn child, who could be a person someday. And this poor mother knows that even if she goes through with an abortion, she might be haunted by it for the rest of her life. He paused again, holding my gaze as I struggled to not look away. It's an awful choice that young woman faces, he said. And no one else should decide it for her.

That didn't change my mind, but it made my own voice sound shrill, and I sensed, in a crowd of my peers, that Mr. Williams had won the upper hand. And even though I believed his position was wrong, I could see not only that he believed what he said, but that he understood how I might feel the way I did. By showing this to others, he disarmed me more than he ever would have by taking a harder line. In that moment I knew, beneath the clamor of my own defensive thoughts, what it meant to be a better man.

Each day a little before noon we gathered around Mr. Chambers, our trip leader, to collect our lunch money, which he handed out in little envelopes stuffed with cash. Mr. Chambers was a stocky man with a square jaw and an easy laugh whose philosophy of supervising high school students was mostly to let them do as they pleased. Once we had our cash for lunch, we were free to pile relish high on hot dogs at a street vendor's cart, or duck into an Indian buffet, or peer at an overhead menu in a Korean restaurant and order by pointing at a photo of the dish we preferred. Some afternoons Mr. Chambers turned us loose in Chinatown or Georgetown, letting us wander the streets in pairs, so long as we made our way back to the bus by our rendezvous time.

Aside from the homeless men rattling coins in Styrofoam cups, some missing arms or legs, others scanning our faces with milky, sightless eyes, we saw a bustling city lined with cherry trees about to burst into bloom. Mr. Chambers had warned us about panhandlers, how some might spend their change on drugs rather than food. But one afternoon I happened upon a man with a curly red beard and no legs, sitting on a wool blanket with his back propped against a stone wall, and even though I knew I was

60

to stay strong and look the other way, his misery called out as he raised his cup of coins and locked my eyes in silence. As I dropped the rest of my lunch money in his mug, I could smell his despair. I knew it wasn't enough, wouldn't matter in the long run, and I walked away into the sunny afternoon with an iron cloud over my thoughts. When I rejoined the group on the bus, climbing the stairs into the happy buzz of talk, I sat stone-faced for many moments, staring out the window at the streaming traffic as I considered how mindless I'd been of those whose stars were falling in the night sky.

It was a sweet-sour feeling, a brief spell of sadness mixed with self-pity that I mistook for compassion, and it lifted as the bus groaned forward and I let myself drift back into the hubbub of talk. We were on our way to a dinner theater, a place called the West End, where the waiters slipped into costume as soon as our steaks and milkshakes had been served and took the stage for *Grease* in jeans and white T-shirts with cigarette boxes rolled up in their sleeves, hair gleaming with gel. I munched my steak and fries as the group belted out "Greased lightning, go greased lightning," and by intermission, when the waiters worked the room again, filling our glasses and taking orders for dessert, I had completely forgotten the man on the street.

On the flight home at the end of the week, as we lifted off over the city, floating westward above the green-and-yellow patchwork of the plains, I believed I'd been changed. Among my early memories of the timbered north woods, red-faced preachers, and dusty baseball fields, I now saw the Lincoln Memorial, the National Mall, and the rolling hills of Arlington Cemetery, where the eternal flame for John F. Kennedy blazed in a disc of rough-cut stone and where many of the hundreds of thousands of soldiers I had presented in my debate as clusters of stick figures lay beneath rows of white headstones. These scenes weren't just photos I saw in books, they were part of my own history now. As we descended over the mountains and touched down, the road back to Troy seemed new, the pines and aspens and mossy firs I'd always taken for granted as the backdrop of my life now arching over the highway with fresh wildness, which I reimagined in terms of the grandeur I'd seen in the city, the mountains rising on all sides like the peak of the Capitol Dome or the Washington Monument's marble spire.

The week in Washington, all those afternoons roaming the streets unsupervised, taught me I could survive beyond my hometown. And even though I'd attended public school for most of my life and had my teachers to thank for the Close Up program, even though fundamentalist doctrine had mostly taught me guilt and self-doubt, I thought faith was so important I never once considered a public university as I began my college search. After narrowing it down to a few Bible schools I pictured as eastern and vaguely refined, I settled on one with the simple logo of a cross on a shield, a Presbyterian college with just over six hundred students, nestled in the Appalachian foothills of Tennessee.

———————

Graduation Day was clear and bright, the kind of spring day in Montana when the sun on my face felt like summer even as the breeze in the shade sent gooseflesh rippling over my neck. We stood on the stone steps of the auditorium, just fifty-two of us, squinting into the midday light as the cameras flashed. Maybe half of us had our eyes set on college: a few headed to West Point, Boston University, and Cornell and many more to the public universities in Missoula and Bozeman. Others would join their uncles on a logging crew, tending bar or waiting tables, watching the town sink deeper into poverty. We had all come of age at the end of a logging and mining boom, when the easy jobs felling timber and shoveling ore were drying up, and anybody hoping to stick around Troy was in for hard times. The big ASARCO silver mine had just closed, and the signs of decline spooked many of our teachers into packing up for more solvent schools. That January, Bill Clinton took the oath as the forty-second U.S. president, just before a truck bomb shook a garage below the Twin Towers in New York, claiming six lives. On the opening page of our yearbook, beneath the heading "Remember the Times," a snapshot of our spirit bell mounted on a concrete platform bears a caption that felt as portentous then as it would become: *"For Whom the Bell Tolls.* It tolled for us on . . . and on . . . and on . . ."

But as we gathered in the gymnasium with our families and friends, squeezing into the metal chairs spread over the basketball court, Mr. Faber struck the opening chords of "Love Is" on his keyboard, and the room swelled with hope. Mr. Faber was not leaving town. He would hang on for nearly two decades more, his Toyota pickup in its place at the school every day like a promise that some things need not change. He'd stirred controversy that year for his theater choices, staging *How Reading Came to Nowhere* in the fall, in which the town of Nowhere is restored to a land of reading after escaping the clutches of Maestro Mean, a tyrant who bans the written word. For the spring play he'd chosen *Sticks 'n Stones*, the story of an English teacher who comes under fire when a parent objects to one of his assigned books, rousing a group called Citizens for Decency to lobby for the teacher's removal. If I had been paying attention, I would have realized Mr. Faber was defending those summer mornings I enjoyed with my mother as a child. He was vouching for Toad and Rat and Mole and the pleasure of metaphor, staving off cynicism—ours and his own—by trying to balance the tough questions with a little levity.

I felt a softening toward Mr. Faber as I stood with the choir watching his fingers move over the keys, and I held nothing back when we sang the chorus: "Love breaks the chains, love aches for every one of us. . . ." I could see my mother in the crowd, her face glistening as it had when she read to me from "The Piper at the Gates of Dawn."

In any other context, these would have been saccharine words. Some will still hear them that way, distrusting the mood of any day that brings us and our mothers and fathers to tears. Youth is more easily remembered in absurdity. I hold that memory to the light, wondering how to see it, whether the fire rising along my back as I sang the chorus was real or just a cheap trick of the song, like the moment in a film when the man leans in and the woman melts a little, strings welling up in the background. Or was it exactly right for us, a surge of belief that every young person deserved on that day regardless of what the years held in store? Even if we could not sustain the feeling forever, surely it was real for Mr. Faber, our teacher, as he raised his voice with our own and prepared to let us go.

The feeling lingered after the ceremony as we shook hands and hugged in the warm June sun, blinking beside our spirit bell. If I had occasionally sparked the ire of my classmates, goading them with my certainties, they forgave it all. "After many years of arguing, we're still friends," one girl wrote in my yearbook. "I'm going to miss our discussions. God bless." My grandparents were there in their dresses and suits. My sister and my mother took turns holding my baby brother, just a few months old, spruced up in a tiny white shirt. I remember the weight of my father's arm on my shoulder, the firm pressure of his hand that held no rebuke. After the photos I loosened my tie and unbuttoned my collar, sighing as the starch fell away from my skin. I was nearly a college boy now, ready to fly out to Tennessee and curl up with a stack of books, reading, reading, as I had always longed to do.

Before I squeezed into the family car and drove away, Mr. Faber pulled me aside and slipped me a thin volume bound in red leather, *My Utmost for His Highest*, a book with a devotional meditation for each calendar day. He'd inscribed it, "To Josh, a man of conviction." I want to believe he saw me then as the best teachers see their students, keeping no record of wrongs, hoping all things. When he shook my hand, patting my back as I turned to go, neither of us could speak, and was it not love, surely love, that made the spring day shimmer and blur?

PART TWO

SIX

Dogwood

A sunny afternoon in Tennessee, late August. The first day of baseball practice. The team is spread along the left field line playing catch, a dozen balls flying back and forth, snapping like popcorn in a kettle. The field sits at the base of a hill below the gymnasium and Liston Hall, the men's dormitory, a five-floor brick fortress built into the slope. The trees are thick with leaves, great sycamores and white oaks and cottonwoods shading the west side of the dorm. Beyond right field, where the grass angles up to the foul pole, the trees cluster in a narrow wood running between the dorm and a golf course. Carts sputter over the greens at the edge of the forest, and in the distance the ping of a driver off the tee rises above the pop of baseballs against leather.

I'm tossing with Jackson, my roommate, a lanky outfielder from North Carolina. He's throwing heat, bruising the inside of my palm when I'm too slow. Sweat beads on my forehead, streaking my cheeks. The chatter is like nothing I've ever heard.

"Atta kid—bring it, son."

"Aw-ight, now—c'mown now."

"Fahr in the hole, bo-ah—at's a way."

Our coach paces the outfield grass, hands clasped behind his back as we throw. He is a short, bandy-legged man with a black moustache who insists we call him Johnny V. Everyone has nicknames. The barrel-chested third baseman with skinny legs is Papaw. The centerfielder, a strong silent type with a giant nose, is Magpie. Newbies go by their surnames until initiated. Hodges. Baker. Lewis. But because my name is difficult to pronounce, within minutes I am southernized as Dooley.

Dooley. It's an invitation to a double life, a name I can shrug on and off with my uniform. I don't like the sound of it, the sloppy, slovenly tone. It isn't how I see myself. But it's all I hear for the rest of the afternoon as I scoop grounders and chase down fly balls and hustle through wind sprints while Johnny V chirps on his whistle. Dooley. Dooley.

These southern boys like the way it feels on their tongues, and they toss it among themselves like they're playing catch. Dooley. O'Doul's. Dooley-kid. I'm popular now, like a pet dog, but I'm not sure I want to be. The air is heavy against my face. The dirt is a deep red, and there is a musty, tangy scent in my nose. I'm still not sure exactly where I am.

It has only been a few days, but it feels like months ago when I left home, riding with my family across the Idaho Panhandle to catch my flight in Spokane, my mother and sister crying quietly, my brother, just seven months old, sleeping in the car seat beside me as I gazed at the pastures and power lines and forest spinning by, the tires humming along the great dark water of Lake Pend Oreille outside Sandpoint. Part of me already ached for home, for the smell of elk steak sizzling in garlic, for the sanctuary of my basement room, cool in summer and snug in winter, firewood crackling in the cast-iron stove. But I was ready to shrug off my parents' grip, eager to flee the long Bible readings at meals and the evening prayers, when the family would kneel around my parents' bed, holding hands, each of us speaking in turn until my father began a rambling monologue, time creaking by until he said, "Our Father," and the rest of us chimed in for The Lord's Prayer.

Yes, I was ready to leave most of that behind. I sent some boxes ahead to the college address, packed with my mother's bear claw quilt, sheets, and extra clothes. I had an enormous suitcase stuffed with the rest of my things, a carry-on backpack crammed with books and school supplies, and my Alvarez guitar. I'd have a week of baseball practice before classes began, by which time I expected to be settled in with a new circle of friends. I did not expect that within a few months I would feel the first pangs of what I believed to be love or that I would be so drunk I could not stand or that I would be laughing by a campfire in the Appalachian woods, my lungs burning from reefer smoke. I hugged my parents and my sister at the gate, swallowed the lump in my throat as I held my brother for a few moments, watching him chortle and slobber in my arms, and then

I gave him back to my mother, hooked my thumbs in my pack straps, and boarded the plane.

Now I'm in Bristol, Tennessee, a town of about thirty thousand—small, by all rights, but still more than thirty times as large as my native Troy. I liked the name Bristol when I read college brochures. It sounded English to me, more eastern than southern, and the campus photos showed brick buildings and bespectacled professors in tweedy jackets, the way I imagined the Ivy League. I did not know Bristol was the birthplace of country music or an annual destination for NASCAR fans who clogged the streets with their buses and mobile homes, tripling the town's population in a single weekend at the local raceway. I was unprepared for the shock when I first arrived on campus, weary from nearly twelve hours of travel, and saw an enormous Confederate flag blazing from a window on the ground floor like a fire from an enemy camp.

Dooley. Dooley. It rings in my head like a song I can't stop humming. Dooley. Dixie. Dooles. In a few weeks I will surrender to it. I will begin to understand country music, and on road trips I will even sit in the back of the van with Hodges, waiting for our favorite song on the radio, the steel guitar swelling as we warble the opening line with Confederate Railroad, "Daddy never was the Cadillac kind." But on the first day of baseball practice it's too new. I don't know who this Dooley kid is. I'm not sure I want to know. I don't think he should take my place.

At the end of practice, our pants streaked with clay, faces grimy with sweat, Papaw hooks his arm around my neck and says, "Atta boy, Dooles. Yer awl raht." And though part of me is still holding back, it seems the only thing to do is clap my hand on his shoulder and walk up the steep hill to the dorm.

When classes begin the following week, I'm ready to starch some shirts, crack the books. This is the real me, the lawyer-to-be who wants to write for the school newspaper and play guitar in the chapel band and keep his nose clean. This is the man I thought I was when I left home. Serious. Focused. Unwavering.

I take notes until my hand cramps in my New Testament survey, trying to keep up with the energetic professor, a trim, balding man pacing the room in a sweater vest. It says McClanahan on the course schedule, but he insists we call him Dr. Mac. He scandalizes us one day by dropping his Bible on the floor, mounting it like a stair, and proclaiming with his arms raised, "I am not standing on the Word of God." A girl in the back of the room gasps. Blasphemy. He goes on to tell us the Word of God is alive, thriving in our hearts, not confined to words on a page. For the first time I begin to wonder how truth can survive so many translations, why Matthew, Mark, Luke, and John all tell slightly different stories about Christ. I've memorized much of the Bible from my father's daily readings and years of church services, but I've never examined the process of canonization, how each book came to be authorized by the early Christian church. I've never heard of the Apocrypha or scholarly debates about whether Jesus' famous charge to the crowd about to stone an adulterous woman, "Let he who is without sin cast the first stone," was really part of the original Gospel of John.

I've been raised to think there are the washed and the unwashed, the redeemed and the lost. But if I can't trust every word in the Bible, surely I can't trust what I feel God might be speaking to me through it. I think of the revival preachers back home who start their sermons claiming God has given them "a word," a divine light that has washed over the page as they've read and filled their heart to overflowing. But what does that personal revelation mean, I wonder, if the words themselves can't be trusted to have been plucked, whole, from the dust and rubble of history?

The questions keep coming in my Western Literature class when we begin reading *The Confessions of St. Augustine*. Torn between lust and his destiny, Augustine pleads with God, "Grant me chastity and continency, but not yet." The way down is the way up, my instructor says. Only by really bottoming out, really rubbing his face in corruption, can Augustine truly be redeemed. I don't think I agree. Where's the personal responsibility? And yet I can feel it happening to me every afternoon on the baseball field, every night in the dorm, every time I answer to Dooley, as if part of me is sliding down a broad path while the other part strains for the straight and narrow way.

I feel myself slip a little further when I fall for my Spanish professor, a tiny woman in her late thirties from Pamplona whom we call Profesora, though I secretly think of her by her first name, Susana. She wears black pantsuits, bright red lipstick, and shirts with enormous white collars hanging open at the neck. La Profesora keeps us laughing, mocking our accents in an exaggerated southern drawl. "Noooo Americanoooo," she cries when our eyelids droop after lunch. I take Juan as my Spanish name for the semester and sit at the front of the class and stay after to chat with Ana, La Profesora's language assistant from Uruguay. Ana walks the halls like she is dancing salsa, all hips and breasts. I am mesmerized by her laugh, which sounds like liquor poured from a bottle, and sometimes I meet her outside her dorm and we talk deep into the night. La Profesora's office smells like chili powder and perfume, and when she and Ana are both there, chattering *en español*, my chest swells as if it might burst, blood throbbing in my ears. But it's not like me to lose control like this. Who am I? I don't recognize myself.

———

Jackson and I clash from the start. He is a good old boy with brown curly hair and a winning smile, always ready for a laugh, and we might be friends if we weren't sharing space. The top of his dresser overflows with free packets of shaving cream and toothpaste and deodorant that our Resident Assistant handed out when we moved in. Jackson mooched extras up and down the hall, gathering a whole nest of the crinkly plastic bags, which now cascade onto the tile floor in the middle of the night, jolting me awake, my throat stiff with alarm.

Most nights I wake to find Jackson's bed empty. He is always out clubbing, so often slipping into bed before dawn and waking at dinnertime to button a silk shirt and do it all over again that he comes to be known as The Vampire. He is a scholarship player, and I reason with him that he is throwing it all away. "Nah," he says. "I always come through in the clutch."

But near the end of the term the only class he's passed is Tennis, which leaves him ineligible even for academic probation. He is still smiling when he leaves before Christmas, crushing my knuckles in his stealth handshake, slipping his thumb over my fingers and bearing down before I have a chance to react. As I lift my throbbing hand in farewell, he hunches into his red Thunderbird and gives it the gas, tires squealing out of the dorm parking lot.

Even before Jackson flunks out, I grow weary of baseball hall, music thumping through the walls late at night, plastic Coke bottles half-full of tobacco juice sitting near the overflowing trashcan in the bathroom for our janitor, Luther, to collect in the morning. Sometimes an airy track with a thumping bass line drifts down the hall, and I know others are flocking to the sound, cramming into the room to watch porn, a communal practice I cannot comprehend. It's like locker-room talk, a chance to swagger and brag in the face of nakedness, pretending to be untouched by what each of us craves. I start making new friends, playing guitar with a few older guys who wear corduroys and Birkenstocks. They have an unofficial fraternity called the King College Mountain Men, the Kappas for short, a porous brotherhood allowing interlopers like me to tag along on weekend hikes and overnight bivouacs near a ramshackle barn where they smoke cigarettes and sometimes wander into the woods, smelling like burning grass when they return to the campfire, a little happier than before. I like talking to them then. Time falls away as we ponder the mysteries of free will or the gender of God, the logs snapping and smoldering to coals. The Kappas all have nicknames, too: Kip, Bubb, Loomis. And even though they know me as Dooley, which seems destined as my southern name, their horizons feel wider than the baseball team's.

———————

Autumn comes and goes in an explosion of color like nothing I've ever seen in Montana, every tree in the Appalachian hills flaming into orange or yellow or red that looks, in early morning, like the alpenglow. Then, suddenly, the trees are bare, the bright forest turning to a thicket of sticks. I keep hitching rides with the Kappas on the weekends, choking on one of Bubb's cigarettes one night, trying the hippie thing on for size. And sometimes there are girls.

One clear night I see her draped in her sleeping bag beside the campfire. Her name is Maya. She is shy and wears long, loose skirts and sweaters in earth tones, her straight brown hair often covering her eyes. Perhaps it is her silence calling to me, or the way, when she pulls her hair away from her cheeks and smiles, it is like a stream flashing among the fallen leaves. I see no pretense in her face. Her cheeks are smooth, without powder, her lips full of their natural bloom.

A longing rises within me. An ache. My whole body is weak with it. I try to gaze into the fire, to lose myself in the snap and dance of the flames, but my eyes keep wandering back to her, back to the shadows playing over her lips, her melancholy eyes. She seems cloaked in reverie. It is a remoteness in her, a sense she is present but not present, that I recognize within myself. Maya reminds me of the women who laughed with my mother around bonfires when I was a child, their long hair falling freely or woven into thick braids. And I wonder now if these first pangs of what I imagine as love might be a yearning for home.

Others join us at the fireside, bottles in hand, cigarettes glowing against the darkness. As they chatter and laugh, I squint against the smoke burning in my eyes and try to keep my gaze from Maya. But I can feel her there, quiet and still, as if she is waiting for me. I begin to believe she is.

It feels like more than a crush. For weeks I hunger for her from afar, watching Maya glide across the college green in her patchwork skirts, running her hand along the backs of her legs as she slides into a desk in our history class. When I think now of the Fertile Crescent or the rise of democracy, I can still see the brown cascade of Maya's hair as she bends over her notebook. My imagination runs so wild it is as if the professor, a short man who rubs his hands together like a squirrel worrying a nut and sometimes rises to the tips of his toes as he speaks, is narrating a film with Maya playing the female leads. In my mind she becomes Cleopatra, Hildegard, Joan of Arc, women made more alluring by their inaccessibility, their power over men.

The hunger gnaws at me day and night. Twisting in my sheets until the blanket chokes me, I try to beat back the ache. This isn't why I've come to college. This isn't part of the plan. I'm supposed to major in Political Science, bat cleanup for the baseball squad, and rack up the résumé I need for a top law school. I'm supposed to be the one calling the shots. But the yearning grips me like nothing I've felt before. It is gooseflesh when I wake and pounding ribs when I lie down, a thickness in my throat whenever I see her.

I begin knocking on doors in the dorm, sitting for hours on the cold tile floor trying to explain what is eating me up. "So ask her out," someone says. "Christ, she's just a girl." But she is more than that to me. I can't say where she is leading me or why. I know only that I feel a pull I can't resist. More and more I feel split between two selves I don't recognize. This dreamy self longing for his lady, wrapped in a cloud of chaste desire, is the part of me that still believes in truth even in the face of questioning, the searcher or quester in me. Though I wonder now if Dooley is another version of the pilgrim, like Augustine or the prodigal son, wallowing down through his own muck to the bedrock from which he can only rise, redeemed.

Friday night. Late November. I'm sitting in Baker's room sipping a Lynchburg Lemonade, watching him play Nintendo football with his roommate, Lewis. They built a plywood loft for their mattresses before they moved in, and they've packed a couch and a television beneath the loft, along with a medium-sized fridge where the rest of my drinks are chilling. As I drain the bottle and heave myself off the floor to get another, I feel a shiver of guilt. Scarcely two months away from home, and it has already come to this. I'm living up to my nickname. Becoming Dooley.

The drinking isn't such a surprise. Even though I steered clear of parties in high school, I had a beer now and then while hunting with my grandfather. I even sipped a little Jägermeister with Jackson earlier in the year, and he succeeded in getting me buzzed one night by filling shots at my elbow while I was studying for a New Testament exam, the temptation of Christ and the Beatitudes finally swimming before my eyes.

It isn't the drinking, it's the getting drunk that feels wrong, and the scheming to bring it about. King College is a dry campus, and we are mostly underage, so a lot of planning goes into a Friday night binge. Baker and Lewis and I pool our funds and beg Papaw or one of the other seniors to make a run with us, and if they can't be swayed, sometimes I talk Cain into letting me borrow his driver's license. Cain is about my height and weight and he is also blond, and if I memorize everything on his license, I can get past the skeptical cashiers, who sometimes quiz me about the home address or Social Security number on the card, which I have come to think of as my own. It is unnerving how easily I have slipped into this role, how unflinchingly I can hold the cashier's gaze while claiming to be someone else.

Then we pull into the back parking lot, stuffing the bottles in our backpacks and baseball duffels to smuggle into the dorm. Lewis leaves first, then Baker, then I follow at a safe distance, my hands in my pockets, back stiff to keep the bottles from rattling. Once inside, we turn the stereo up, grinning as we unload our packs.

Tonight I plan to drink whiskey. It is a calculated self-destruction, like my weightlifting routine. I want to see how far I can tear myself down, what shreds of reason might linger in my thoughts, whether my mind will still be my own then or whether I will be easily swept into some other vice. An experiment, I tell myself. A little data gathering is all.

The lemonades go down easy, and then I start in on the Jim Beam, drinking straight from a pint bottle, each fiery swallow easier than the last. My chest burns, my face humming with blood. Lewis and Baker fade into the background as I sit on the floor with my back against the cement wall. After draining one pint of bourbon, I start another. The loft wheels overhead. My vision narrows as if I'm gazing through the wrong end of a telescope. I slouch a little lower on the wall, my arms lying like sandbags at my sides. Sure enough, I'm still in here. If I close my eyes, my head whirls like a carnival ride, but I feel strangely calm, as if my body is falling away, as if my thoughts are music and an unseen hand is turning the volume down, down, down, to silence.

———

I'm in the bathroom, kneeling before a toilet. Lewis and Baker are struggling to hold me up, their hands hooked under my arms. The place reeks of sour whiskey. Something is floating in the water, splattered over the seat. Then my belly spasms and I'm heaving bile, my head and chest and arms gone slack.

———

Whispering. We're in the hallway. It's dark except for the footlights. I can feel my toes dragging, my arms wrapped over Lewis' and Baker's shoulders. Someone is digging in my pocket for my key, and then we're at my door. Baker grunting as he drops me onto my bed, the springs creaking under my weight. The soft click of the door.

———

Morning. Nearly noon. My head is pounding, vomit crusted to the side of my mouth where I must have hurled again in the night. I make my way down to the shower, squinting in the glare of the light against the white tile. It hurts to move, but it feels good to soap up and soak in the heat. I'm still unsteady on my feet, and the walk back to my room puts me to sleep until dinnertime, when I wake faint from hunger, my head still splitting, throat cracked and dry.

And when I finally sober up, when my headache finally clears after two wasted days lying in the dark in my room, what have I learned? I feel embarrassed to be sick, sorry for flaking out on Lewis and Baker, though they tell me they've been there, too, everyone has at one time or another. But strangely the guilt is gone. I've gone down into the darkness and found nothing there, no raging lust waiting to be unleashed. Not even a rock bottom, just a vague squalor to be shrugged off before moving on.

This Dooley kid was not part of my plan. But maybe he isn't so different from me after all. Maybe he is just the counterweight I need to bring me down to earth.

———————

Late November. Evening. I'm strumming my Alvarez, sitting cross-legged on my bed, the room dark but for the soft light of my desk lamp. Jackson is out clubbing, drinking Zima at Tu La Fe, his favorite dance club. I run through a few blues riffs I've learned by ear and play a little "Jet Airliner" and "Proud Mary." Collective Soul, a Georgia band, has dominated the radio lately, and I try to puzzle out the chords to "Shine." I like the resistance of the strings, the solid feel of a bar chord against the fret board. I like the word "fret," how it captures the feeling that drives me to play, groping for order up and down the neck of the guitar.

I've been playing a lot lately while thinking of Maya, but none of the songs I know give voice to her hold on me. I can't quite get the Collective Soul riff down, but I start to hear something else, a new song, as I'm fumbling with the chords. My finger slips on the A chord, and there is dissonance with the top strings open, a tension like the tightness in my chest. I put down my flat pick and start trying it out with my fingers, my thumb keeping time with the bass string, and my other fingers walking up and down the chord. I've never written a song before, but I start humming a note that sounds right, and then I cast around and find E minor. I try it a few times, walking down the neck from the open A, and the melody falls into place, rising a little, then falling down to E minor like the sound of yearning itself. Her name fits the rhythm, and I sing, "Ma-ya June, Ma-ya June—what can I say to you, Ma-ya June, Ma-ya June?"

I stop for a moment, embarrassed by the sound of my own voice. A techno beat thumps down the hall. My computer fan whirs on the desk. After a spell I try again, softly. And the whole song comes together. I can hear it, how the verse moves between the suspended and minor chords, how the chorus should swell to a major note before falling back to the minor, like a struggle between sadness and hope. I lean over to my desk and slide my notebook onto my lap and scribble out the lyrics, struggling with the chorus. "Come morning rain, revive my heart again," it goes, "Come morning sunshine, fill me with your light. Come evening breeze, whisper softly to me why in the morning dew I see Maya June."

Now when I remember those words and the young man writing them down, I cringe a little, the way I do in a crowd when a performer makes a mistake. It's the kind of memory I'm tempted never to tell, too raw and too close to the man I am now, the kind Dooley wants to grind under his heel in disgust. But it is the beginning of understanding writing as a form of searching, a crying out in hope of reply.

I never sing the song for Maya. When she starts seeing someone else, I know I've lost my chance, and after a few weeks of heartache the feeling slowly fades. I play it once for the Kappas, and Kip and Bubb switch on their analog recorder to catch it the second time. But it sounds silly by then, so I swap "Kathmandu" for "Maya June" and sing it that way. When I start playing in coffee shops later on, the story is always good for a laugh, how I had this serious crush on a girl and thought I was in love but then had to change the words after someone else snatched her up. "Kathmandu," I croon, "What can I say to you?" I smile as I sing, and people laugh as they sip their coffee, snug in their wool socks, Rasta hats, and Birkenstocks. But there's something prayerful in the tune that still triggers an old, buried hope whenever I think of her name.

The semester winds down, and I survive my first finals week, cramming late into the night until my eyes slam shut and I fall forward into my notebook, waking with my cheek pressed to the page. I try a few caffeine pills, but they make me so jangly and strung out the next day that I decide to allow myself at least a few hours of sleep each night. The room feels empty without Jackson's pile of laundry, but I like the quiet and shut myself away to study, shrugging off the warm cloak of sleep as I try to recall all the dates and names and events of western civilization, my thoughts swimming with history.

Then exams are done, and my room feels empty as I pack for the holiday. I sleep all the way to Atlanta and snooze on the flight to Salt Lake, waking to see the snowy peaks of the Wasatch Mountains rising over the city and the great lake beyond. As the plane banks in from the south for the landing, I'm pressed to the window, lit up by the open space of the salt flats and the rim of ridgelines and peaks. I know there is much I can't go home to anymore, much that has fallen away in five short months, but there is no forgetting this western landscape. And when the little commuter plane eases down into the Flathead Valley, nestled beneath the Rocky Mountain chain stretching up into Canada, I feel a wild stab of joy.

My parents meet me at the gate with my sister and my little brother, who has grown considerably since I left, nearly a year old now. I put down my guitar and hug them all. We are shy with each other on the drive home, my mother and sister drifting to sleep while I watch the dark forest flashing along the highway, the river buried in snow and ice. When we're quiet like this I can let most of the changes drop away and feel like a boy again, dreaming in the back seat, soaking up the rise and fall of the road.

But as soon as we unload the car and I carry my things to my room and we sit down at the table, joining hands for a prayer and watching the steam rising from the mashed potatoes and elk steak and mushroom gravy as my father drones through a Bible chapter, I feel my new selves crowding into my throat. My parents listen, brows knitted, as I talk about my New Testament class. This is what they were afraid of, I can see it in their eyes. *Brainwashed*, they're thinking. *Our boy is slipping away.* So I ask them how they explain the discrepancies between the Gospels or how they know which parts of the Bible are still true and which were meant for a certain time and place. Should we still stone disobedient children? I ask, carving my steak. Should we kill those who work on the Sabbath? I don't know why I'm so angry, why I'm taking it out on them. My father mutters something about the substance of things hoped for, the evidence of things not seen. My mother busies herself with my baby brother in his highchair.

I want them to acknowledge that I'm still their son, even though I no longer pretend to follow along. I want to bang the table and shout, I don't know who I am yet, but I'm trying to find out, I'm searching. I want them to say they'll love me no matter what, and deep down I know that is true. But all I can feel now is their fear of who I've become, so I hush and bend again to the cold potatoes and the mushroom gravy congealing on my plate. And when the holiday ends, when I pack for the spring term and hug my family goodbye again at the gate, I am ready to go.

I don't know it yet, but this is the beginning of more than a decade of running away from my past while stubbornly holding onto it, never going anywhere to stay, always uprooting myself. It's a curious mixture of sorrow and relief as I board the plane to face my second college term, heavy with the knowledge that my family and I can only diverge from this point forth. Yet the farther I wander in the wide world beyond these alpine lakes and talus slopes and great cedar trees, the tighter the pull of the place on my heart grows, even as every time I try to come home I must face what drove me away from the start.

———

It's early March, and we're back on the baseball field playing catch before practice. Jackson is gone, so I'm tossing with Hodges. He is a stout redhead, and a few of the guys called him Ginger for a while, but it didn't stick. His name seems to suit him perfectly, so that's who he is on the field and off. Hodges. No more, no less. I'm impressed by his elusiveness. These southern boys can catch you with their words like a frog nabbing flies. "Hey sawed-off!" they yell at short opposing pitchers. When a runner trips in front of our dugout, sprawling headfirst in the dust, they holler "Sniper!" and duck as if a gunman is picking them off from long range. You might be sprinting for a fly ball lofted into the gap in the outfield, closing ground but looking like you might have to dive, and they'll shout "Git nekked!" And then even if you leap and skid on your chest and come up with the ball, everyone has just had a fleeting thought of you laid out bare-assed in midair. It's the feeling I had the first time I answered to Dooley, as if some joker had just tugged my pants down.

I'm a little jealous of Hodges. Once you have a nickname, there's no shrugging it off. Our first baseman, Kleinman, a tall, gaunt fellow obsessed with Great Danes, is pegged as Kleindog, then just Dog. Another tall, freckled kid from Cohutta, Georgia, is dubbed Hutta and must carry the name of his hometown wherever he goes. It's a kind of tribalism, this naming, a form of control. You are who we say you are, the namers imply. My parents wanted me to be the stalwart champion of Israel, Joshua marching around Jericho. To seal the covenant my mother bought me a framed interpretation of my name's origins, derived from the Hebrew word for salvation and translating roughly as "Jehovah saves." According to some, the name Jesus is a variant of Joshua. It's a long way down from there to Dooley, but I'm making my peace with it, tossing with Hodges on the spring grass.

Hodges and I survived our ritual hazing in the fall, when the upperclassmen made us wear dresses and hold hands as they smeared cow shit on our faces like eye black and marched us to the girls' dorm singing "You Are My Sunshine." Hodges is content to bide his time as we both warm the bench through the spring season. But when I watch Papaw strike out or let a grounder trickle between his legs at third base, I fume in my seat.

Between innings one day Cain offers me a pinch of Skoal snuff. I accept out of boredom, unprepared for the wave of nausea and the sudden buzz. I sit next to Hodges for another inning, my head spinning, before I rinse out my mouth. But the next game I'm at it again, bumming a dip from Cain and trying to last as long as I can—two, three innings—then tossing the wad in the grass and trying not to gag as I wash the taste from my teeth, my throat burning with it. By the end of the spring I'm hooked, buying my own snuff, jonesing for it in the middle of class. It's a way to swallow my disappointment, surrendering to my place on the bench. I pack my lip with snuff and worry the plug with my tongue and try to forget what I know, that the game is slipping away, that I'm losing my grip on the dream. When I wash my mouth out, the taste is still there, like bile in my throat after a long night of retching.

———————

More and more I drift away from the team even though I keep suiting up for the games. I'm tired of missing class for road trips and smuggling booze for the endless party in the dorm. On the weekends I wander the Appalachian Trail with the Kappas, driving through Damascus, Virginia, hiking past the grassy saddle at Massie Gap, where wild ponies graze, and climbing Mount Rogers, thirsty for a view from the top. It is late spring, and the hillsides are greening, gentle ridgelines fading into a blue haze on the horizon. The cool air and rocky knobs at the summit remind me of Montana peaks. But I tell Loomis and Bubb these are mere hills compared to the country I come from. Kip smiles. He is a tall, rangy guy who hikes faster in sandals than anyone else in our group can in boots. He has a quiet authority, so I listen when he tells me it's an old mountain range, almost four hundred million years older than the Rockies I still think of as home. An ancient place, I think. But tame all the same.

That night, or one of those nights in the woods as we're staring into the campfire, I try a drag or two on the joint making its way around the circle. It's one of the taboos I thought I would never cross, but I've been watching the Kappas smoke it all year, and it only makes them quiet and ponderous and gentler than they already are. *Another experiment*, I think, *another stage of the quest*. I cough as I try to hold onto each drag, my lungs burning from the smoke and the heat. But it gets easier each time, and it seems like the weed keeps circling the fire, as if someone has rolled another bone. Three or four or five times I breathe deep and pass it on, holding each pull until my throat tickles and I cough out the smoke.

It doesn't seem like much. I keep waiting for a high or some sign I'm on drugs, but we're all just gazing into the fire the way we always do, watching the flames dance as the logs snap and settle, sparks floating into the night. I sink a little deeper into the fire. I think of the home place, of my parents when I was young, when my mother invited friends over with their spinning wheels, brushing the raw wool between wooden paddles with stiff tines until the ball of fiber was smooth and light, like a white, puffy cloud, like the center of the flame transfixing me.

Dooley's stoned, someone says. And I look up and come back to myself and the ring of friendly faces grinning in the fire's glow. Am I? I ask, a little too gleefully. Am I really? Someone laughs and soon everyone is cracking up, and I'm lying on my side, my face pressed against the cold leaves, and it seems I've never heard anything funnier in my life. I can feel part of myself pull back from the scene, watching my sides heave. I've come a long way from the buttoned-down boy who thought he had his future mapped out.

I'm still not sure exactly who I am, still code-switching between the baseball team and the Kappas and my classes, wondering what it means to be a Christian if I can't be certain of everything. But I'm learning how to live with unanswered questions, how to try on ideas knowing I might change my mind. I've been thinking about Saul on the road to Damascus, how he was so certain of his purpose before he was struck blind and transformed into Paul. It's much like the cave in Plato's allegory of the man chained to see only shadows, how his understanding of the world blossoms gradually once he is released, how even in the daylight he can never gaze directly into the sun. I'm learning the way of the pilgrim, the restless, endless search.

———————

As spring swells into bloom on campus, the buds on the dogwood trees open to flowers in the shape of a cross, four petals, each with a notch stained pink at the tip. There is a legend about the dogwood tree claiming it was the wood used to build the cross where Christ was crucified. It was a larger tree then, tall and strong, as the story goes. But the dogwood pitied Christ as he hung there waiting to die and begged his forgiveness for its part in his suffering. He felt compassion for the tree, making its branches grow crooked and thin, so it could never again be used to take a man's life. To this day the tree's petals bear the stain of the nails, where Christ's hands bled into the wood, and the stamen at the center of each blossom grows in a cluster recalling the crown of thorns.

This is part of college lore, the story behind the Dogwood Festival every April, when each class elects a couple to represent them at the formal ball, and the whole college selects a King and Queen. It's our version of homecoming, alumni gathering on their old stomping grounds for the weekend to cheer on the teams and take in the spring musical. I watch them from the dugout during the baseball game, these strangers in the stands with their penny loafers and slicked-back hair. I wonder where they come from and what they're trying to get back by coming here, if their lives have unfolded as they've planned or if any of them have been withered by circumstance, brought a little closer to earth like the dogwood tree. I work the tobacco deeper into my lip and stare at the men in their spring blazers and the women in their yellow dresses, and I wonder what stories they have to tell.

SEVEN

Alberta

While some of my college friends buttered popcorn at their local shopping malls during the summer and others moved back to the family farm to cure tobacco, I signed on as a firefighter with the U.S. Forest Service. The fire crew at the Three Rivers District in Troy drew a lot of college kids like me back to our rural hometowns, but there were teachers on our crew, and ski bums who worked only to finance their backcountry treks, and grizzled characters undaunted by the waning timber and mining industries who supported their families by cobbling together seasonal Forest Service work and odd winter jobs. There were men and women as young as eighteen and as old as sixty, gay and straight and bi, rednecks and hippies, future doctors and lawyers and dental hygienists, fundamentalists and atheists, lapsed Catholics and Zen philosophers, cancer survivors, veterans of Vietnam and the Gulf War, and more than a few anarchists. There was a good chance that on any given topic a fair share of us would disagree, yet we forged a tight kinship during those summer months. Whatever squabbling arose eventually fell silent beneath the radiant heat of a backburn or the click of our tools in the dirt.

The Kootenai National Forest is big country, roughly three times as large as Rhode Island. The Three Rivers District alone covers more than half a million acres in the northwest corner of Montana, where the Yaak and Kootenai and Bull River Valleys lie between the Idaho and Canadian borders. Growing up there made me certain I knew the place, but I began to see it differently from the vantage of the fire crew, driving gated roads I'd never explored even on foot, looking down on the valley from peaks I'd only glimpsed from the highway. As I rode shotgun in the fire engine on the way to our prescribed burns, I drank in the cedar and fir trees scraping their boughs along the top of the cab, soaking up the sinuous ridgelines rolling north toward Cranbrook and Calgary.

Summers on the fire crew all run together in my memory as time out of time, and this was especially true of assignments off forest, when a call might come in from Arizona or California or even Canada and a few of us from Three Rivers would ship out with a crew patched together from other districts on the Kootenai. The feeling of holiday from real life intensified in fire camps where we lived in tent villages and worked twelve- or fourteen-hour shifts every day, sometimes straight through the night, lighting a backburn or patrolling the edges of the fire in the dark. It reminded me of *Brigadoon*, a musical I saw in college, which told the story of an enchanted village in Scotland that slipped out of normal time when a minister begged God to shield it from the outside world. Thereafter, the village only appeared for a day every hundred years, its inhabitants just short of eternal youth, living a decade each millennium. It was an apt metaphor for college life, too, since campus was a parallel universe where the usual rules seemed not to apply. What happened in the fire crew stayed there, for the most part, and this prompted some of us to say and do things we might never otherwise have dared.

—————————

It was a cloudy day in June, the first day of my second season at Three Rivers, when we got the call from northern Alberta. The crew was crowded round the chain-link equipment locker in the fire shop, jostling as close to the front of the line as we could in hopes of getting a good pair of Nomex pants and one of the vintage smokejumper packs, when our supervisor stepped into the hallway and shouted, "Jones, Tozzi, Doležal, Jacobson— my office." Lonna Huff had fought her way to assistant fire management officer through the old boy Forest Service. She raised greyhounds and looked a little like one, too. Only rarely did she raise her voice.

I had just gathered my gear and hurriedly signed off with Maddox, who stood with his clipboard near the piles of red packs and green-and-gold fire clothes. Tozzi and Jacobson gave up their places in line, to much hooting and elbow jabbing from the others, and we followed Jones down the hallway to Lonna's office, a tiny paper-strewn space shared by three other supervisors. The bookshelves were jammed with three-ring binders, maps, training workbooks, and odd novels, *Catch-22* and *Vineland* nestled among the thrillers. A tattered poster taped to the door showed a photo of a mime troupe with the caption, "Occupants are lifers with nothing to lose."

Lonna motioned for us to sit. Jones and Tozzi took the open chairs as Jacobson and I leaned against the doorjamb.

"How'd you like to go to northern Alberta?" she grinned. "I just got the call, and we're trying to put together a crew. Libby will send a squad, we'll get one each from Eureka, Rexford, and the Cabinet district, and I thought we could send you four. Jones, you'd be our squad boss. They'll be sending Claude Shanley from the Cabinet to run the crew."

Jones sniffed. "What the hell do they want us in Alberta for?"

"Big muskeg fires, they say. It's a ground moss, grows up to five feet deep. Anytime those swampy areas dry out a little bit, like down in the Everglades, you get some bad fires. Once the heat starts skunking around in that moss, it's almost impossible to stop. Anyway, you guys interested?"

"Hell, yes," Tozzi said. We all agreed. Nobody ever turned down an off-forest assignment. With twenty-one straight days on the clock, twelve to fourteen hours a day, the overtime was reason enough. We were all cash-craving college kids except for Jacobson, one of the Troy boys still determined to make a life for himself in our hometown. Jones and Tozzi stood to go, but Lonna waved them back.

"There's something I want you all to know, just to be on the safe side. Claude is a nice guy, but he's not all there. Just two years ago he was crew boss with a hotshot outfit, and one of his guys died on the fire line—tree-felling accident or something. Whatever it was, it got Claude demoted. If it was me, I'd never send him out again, but it's not my call." Lonna leaned forward in her chair. "You guys don't hesitate to call home if you think things aren't safe up there, OK? No heroics. I need you to pay attention and speak up if your gut tells you to. Alright?"

She looked at Jones to be sure. He nodded and pulled his cap down over his eyes.

We made a quick business of packing our things and drove a green club cab to the Kalispell airport, where we would catch our flight to Edmonton.

Clouds had gathered quickly throughout the day, and rain began to fall as we climbed Whiskey Hill on the outskirts of Libby. Jones drove with one hand on the wheel, the other clutching an empty Mountain Dew bottle against his red wool shirt. His lower lip bulged with a wad of Kodiak snuff. Jones stood over six feet and weighed at least 250 pounds, much of that in his hips. It was hard to read his thoughts. When he saw a woman in tight pants, he was apt to say, "I'd eat a mile of her shit just to see where it came from." But then he might fall into a brooding silence as he did on this drive, the pale daylight gleaming on his glasses, wheel rocking beneath his wrist. Jacobson rode shotgun, listening to country radio. The steady hiss of the tires and the thump of a broken windshield wiper lulled Tozzi and me to sleep in the back seat.

We woke to doors slamming and found ourselves on the tarmac in a desolate part of the Kalispell airport reserved for charter flights. It was scarcely noon, but thunderheads had walled off the sun and the Flathead Mountains, so we could see only the glistening asphalt and the dim outline of the terminals. Jones had his red-and-orange packs slung over each shoulder and was walking quickly toward the concrete warehouse where we were to wait for the rest of the crew to join us. We followed, heads bowed against the rain.

"Jesus and Mary," said Tozzi, once we were inside. "How the hell are we going to fly in this?" Jones shrugged and tossed his gear in the pile that had formed just inside the door. The place reeked of wet boot leather and snuff.

Libby's squad leader, Pat Caspe, rose to greet us. Pat wore a camouflage Mack Truck cap with nylon netting in the back. She was stout and looked like a man from behind, her blond curls bulging beneath her cap. Pat had gone to work in a silver mine after high school. When the mine closed she signed on with a logging company, and now that the timber industry was on the wane, she had fallen back on seasonal work with the Forest Service. She was clearheaded and kind, even though she put up a tough front. I was glad to see her on this crew.

"What's the word, Pat?" Tozzi cupped his hand to his ear.

"Word is, you sleep when you can, eat when you can, and mind your own ass," she said.

A few hours passed, it seemed, before the others arrived. But once the Eureka and Rexford squads rolled in, the Cabinet folks were close behind, and then we got our first look at Claude Shanley. He was a short, potbellied man. His round spectacles had slid halfway down his face in the rain, and his mouth gaped as he tried to hold them up by wrinkling his nose. Pat Caspe and Jones stood to introduce themselves. Soon the other squad leaders followed, forming a knot around Claude. He had a habit of touching his face as he spoke, and he stood with one leg relaxed, his hips in a rakish tilt. I could tell this aggravated Jones, who formed impressions quickly and harbored grudges longer than anyone I knew. He must have been recalling Lonna's warning. *Listen to your gut. Speak up if you have to.*

As the squad leaders broke away, word trickled back that we were going to fly regardless of the storm. The room began to buzz as we crowded to the windows for another look at the sky. Rain was falling in sheets, puddles rippling around the tires of the plane. Lightning glittered on the tarmac. The thunder broke immediately.

Whether it be instinct or bravado or plain stupidity, it is hard not to board a plane when your crewmates are dashing through the rain to toss their packs into the cargo bin. No matter how bald-headed and knock-kneed the crew boss, no matter how uncertain he might seem of his own demands, it is hard to look him in the eye and refuse to follow orders. It is easier to keep your place in line, kvetching all the while, mount the stairs to the plane, and buckle in.

Our fire training stressed safety above all else, steeping us in cautionary tales of crews who overlooked obvious watch-out situations and ended up dead. It was an easy calculus in hindsight. But we never had a class on the unwritten rules of the field, where danger is not always dire. Where does flying into a thunderstorm rank on the scale of acceptable risk? I had some doubts about whether the propellers would be turning now if this were a commercial flight, whether the attendant would be sealing the cockpit door as the engines whined and the plane lurched forward. But there was no bucking it now, so I gripped the armrests and sank into the seat as the ship lifted off, swaying and dipping against the black sky. Gusts shuddered the cabin as we climbed through the storm, air pockets sucking the plane down fifty feet before updrafts shot us skyward again. I watched lightning flash beyond the tip of the wing and tried to swallow my fear.

The next morning, after staying over in Edmonton, we boarded a yellow school bus and headed north toward Slave Lake. Once we left the hayfields in Fawcett and Flatbush, the roadside turned to scraggly pines and firs and the occasional aspen grove. The horizon was a brown ribbon of earth. Tozzi quickly succumbed to the hum of the tires and the mesmeric drift of landscape, his head bouncing on my shoulder. I stayed awake, struck by the sensation of moving north, off my personal map. Troy was scarcely an hour from the border, and though I had crossed many times into British Columbia and Alberta, I had no more notion of the northern reaches of the provinces than a Vancouver dweller might have of Nome.

There was little traffic on the highway, just endless patchy trees. The land was so flat it offered blankness as perspective. When the trees opened up enough for me to see some distance, it was like a glimpse into nothing, and when the fir thickets blocked the view again, I felt dizzy, the way a fisherman might feel walking over a frozen lake after knocking a hole in the ice to discover the water twenty feet below.

We passed a few desolate homes, mostly trailer houses, many abandoned. This prompted some heckling from Bauer, a loudmouth on the Libby squad, who had spontaneously nicknamed Jacobson "Dirt Chicken" and was now intent on making that name stick. It was like the game Slug Bug, which I used to play with my sister on long drives, each of us scanning the oncoming traffic for a Volkswagen Beetle and pummeling the other's arm if we saw one first. Now the game was to spot a trailer and shout "Dirt Chicken!" at Jacobson. "Looks like home, eh?" Bauer would say, and the game would go on.

Jacobson was nearly as tall as Jones, but not as stout. He was fond of denim cowboy shirts with brass snaps and always wore a Husqvarna cap over his greasy mullet. At a distance he might have seemed formidable, but in person he was shy and invited abuse the way an old dog draws mange. I liked Jacobson and thought he got short shrift most of the time, but I was all too glad to forget the dead landscape outside, so I joined in the fun.

We were a sorry crew, truth be told, mostly kids with a season or two of experience. The crew boss trainee from Rexford, who scarcely cleared five feet and maybe weighed a buck thirty, answered to Tadpole. There was Claude, who wore a perpetual grin under his gleaming spectacles and walked like he had to piss. Five women had joined the crew, including Pat Caspe, and they were all solid but for a histrionic blond from Libby. We thought our Troy squad was tough enough, and Craig, the helicopter specialist, knew what he was doing. Still, there was an alchemy from the start that brought out the worst in some of us. Tozzi and I—usually amiable sorts—laughed along with the others when the bus passed another trailer and Bauer led the Dirt Chicken chorus while Jacobson turned a deeper shade of red.

The bus sped northward, deeper into the muskeg country between the Greater and Lesser Slave Lakes. The dirt roads made for slower driving, so it could have been forty or fifty miles before we arrived at the fire camp, which covered one end of an airstrip cut from fir and aspen groves. Yellow canvas tents sat in rows among the gopher holes, each tent supported by peeled poles lashed together in an A-frame. Two sanitation trailers and two portable shower houses stood behind the mess hall, a circle tent of white canvas. There was a medic tent and a trailer set up for the division supervisor and a row of yellow school buses like ours. As we pulled to a stop in the makeshift parking lot, a Jeep rumbled out to meet us. A small, balding man who looked a lot like Claude jumped out and broke open two boxes in the back of the Jeep, which we soon saw held rubber boots and bottles of mosquito spray. Claude stepped from the bus to help, and the two portly men stood on either side of the bus door to dispense the gear as we filed out.

"Looks like we'll be fighting more skeeters than fire," said Bauer. He looked around at the tents. "Damn, Jacobson, you've got your own Dirt Chicken village. It's a redneck fiefdom out here, and you're the king." Bauer made a mock bow, and we all laughed as we stood clutching our boots and repellant. We waited for Claude to give directions about our bunking arrangements, but he climbed into the Jeep and bounced away with the camp administrator, so we carried our packs through the camp, peering under the flaps to see which tents were occupied. Jones and I claimed a vacant tent and began unrolling our sleeping pads. The canvas canopy stank of camphor and mold. Black ants scurried over the dirt floor. As the sun died out on the western horizon and night fell on the camp, we went about arranging a home for ourselves in the dust.

We woke to a tumult of helicopters landing on the airstrip, the *thock-thock-thock* of their blades like a hundred axes driven into wood. They were Type I logging ships with enough space for ten to twelve passengers, and we could feel their power through the ground as we lay in our mummy bags. After the usual briefings, when we heard again that our fire shelters would make no difference in a muskeg fire, owing to the deep ground moss, we lined up on the airstrip with the other crews to await our turn for a chopper ride.

Regulations in the United States demand that crews manifest their loads, which means calculating the weight of everyone and everything on board, but the Canadian rules were more lax. Their pilots encouraged us to pile in, and if the load proved too heavy, they'd just kick someone off. Claude stood on the landing strip with his arms crossed and did nothing to suggest otherwise, which raised some uneasiness among our crew. This was a clear watch-out situation, the kind that flew in the face of the training manuals we all knew, and I could see Jones chewing on his lip as he mulled it over. Claude had a way of standing apart from the group that might have made him seem tough if he had been six inches taller and thicker in the shoulders rather than the paunch. As it was, he looked distracted, even senile. The other crew bosses shepherded their squads into the choppers, leaning in through the doors to make sure everyone was buckled in, but when it was our turn to board, Claude drifted to the back of the line and let us fend for ourselves. Craig, our helicopter specialist, did the best he could to make sure our loads were reasonable, and we all arrived safely at the drop point.

Boarding and dismounting from a large helicopter is breathtaking, the great wash of air like no wind I have ever felt, more like the surge of a river than any breeze. We approached and departed with our heads bowed, as if we were playing parts in a war film, and then we stood back in the trees as we watched the ships lift off, their noses lowered as they whizzed off over the forest. During training sessions we had been taught to hit the ground if a chopper crashed nearby, since the broken blade would hurtle like grapeshot in all directions. Each morning I stood with my legs tensed at takeoff and after landing, imagining the great blade spinning free of its axis and slicing me in two. It was the most exhilarating part of the day.

The rest of the time we passed mopping up, a dull business that drags out for weeks after a big fire has spent itself. We began as a crew, all twenty of us walking straight through the forest in a grid, no more than an arm's length from our nearest neighbor, watching for smoldering hot spots. If we found a pocket of heat, we would call out "Smoke!" and the rest would wait for us to potato-patch the spot, hacking down to mineral soil with the hoe end of our pulaskis, turning the embers under.

Mopping up is a dismal job because it most often occurs in a moonscape of a forest, where the ground is one expanse of ash and the trees look like they have been blasted by the fifth trumpet of the Apocalypse. This fire was different because the charred areas were swampy and half the time we swatted at mosquitoes and gnats while sloshing through the muskeg. Still, we got plenty dirty digging in the char. Ash after a large-scale blaze has a certain energy, flying up your pant legs and coating your teeth, gathering in your hair and clumping like tar at the corners of your eyes.

The hazards of mopping up are small but real. Roots burn up to the bases of trees, leaving little tunnels that let the earth collapse underfoot, sometimes enough to sprain an ankle or slam a knee back into the joint. Many trees teeter on a rootless trunk after a hot ground fire and can topple silently at any time. Cold trailing is part of the job, running a bare hand along the underside of a log to feel for heat. Even when there is no fire in sight, you can still get badly burned by grabbing a branch with live embers or thrusting a hand into a white-hot pocket of ash.

But boredom is a greater hazard, nearly as perilous to a firefighter as pride. Lonna's warning had given us too much pride by entitling us to question the chain of command, and so that was what our thoughts went back to when mopping up grew dull, which made a deadly stew. It was never a question so much of whether we were in danger as whether we could get Claude in trouble for leading us into it. And the more we kicked at the ash and spit it out and ran our sooty hands across our faces, the more we blamed our discontent on him.

The fire had mostly spent itself, so we took long breaks that first week, digging easy chairs for ourselves in the muskeg and dipping snuff. But once the dreariness of the work stole back over us, Claude was much on our thoughts. After the first week we gave up gridding as a crew and wandered about in squads, chopping out a few smoldering stump holes and leaning on our pulaski handles for many minutes afterward, until the mosquitoes drove us back to walking. Jones carried a radio on a yellow chest holster, but we often lost track of where the other squads were until the end of the day, when we tried to find our way back to where the choppers had dropped us that morning. The flat aspen groves made orienteering difficult. Here was a swampy clearing, there was a little clutch of trees, and beyond were other clearings and oily marshes and little stands of fir. During one of our many breaks, I closed my eyes and tried to remember which way was north, and the more I struggled to decide, the more it felt as if the darkness behind my eyes were empty space, as if I were hurtling through the cosmos. Lazy moments like these multiplied as we logged more twelve-hour shifts, rising at dawn to file through the mess line, waiting for the morning briefing, lining up for our chopper ride, then drifting about in the field for ten hours before catching our return flight. The numbing shuffle felt like hunting with no hope of seeing game.

So it was really no surprise when Tozzi stepped behind a tree one day to piss and came tiptoeing back, motioning for us to follow. We crept up a knoll, and there in a little hollow we saw Claude fast asleep, hands folded on his potbelly, cap pulled down over his eyes. Jones smiled the way he used to on the football field, when he planned to dive under the center off the snap and grab at the opposing quarterback's shoelaces. "Damn, I wish I had a camera," he whispered, and we crouched there for a moment deciding what to do. Then Claude stirred in his sleep, and we stole away to ponder what this meant.

"That guy's as crazy as a rat in a tin shithouse," Jones said. "He doesn't have any more sense than Jacobson does." Jacobson mumbled a retort and began chewing on a stem of grass. Tozzi and I agreed. Something had to be done about Claude.

One week turned into two. Then one day we were gridding, sloshing through the muskeg, when we saw thunderheads building in a big cloudbank with a purple belly. By lunchtime the storm had blown overhead, and the temperature had dropped at least twenty degrees. Jones called the other squad leaders and got us all together. Claude heard the radio traffic and joined us. As the sky grew dark, we pulled out our rain shells and ponchos and began hunkering down among a few fir trees that had survived the burn. The air smelled electric, like ozone. Hail began drumming on our hardhats. Lightning flashed in the distance. In that flat country the trees were virtually all the same height, and it seemed that a strike might touch down anywhere.

We waited, peering from beneath the drawn hoods of our ponchos, the wet ground soaking our asses. Our feet grew cold in our rubber boots. Then Claude got anxious and started calling the chopper pilots on his handheld radio. I could not make out what he said, but he must have been pleading for an emergency rescue. Hail can be deadly to helicopters, sometimes breaking windows, doors, or the external pitot tubes that measure airspeed. If hail is large enough, it can bring a ship down, so it surely would have been safer for us to wait out the storm. But Claude got us all to stand and start moving toward an opening a few hundred yards away that turned out to be a power line. We could see the pea-sized hail bouncing from the wires. The right-of-way cut a corridor through the trees, and our ponchos billowed as powerful gusts surged down the line. Lightning snapped once more, the rumble a few seconds behind. Claude's radio squawked and stammered while we waited at the edge of the trees. Jones stood nearby with his arms crossed and his lower lip, full of snuff, bulging from beneath his hood.

Then the broken drone of the choppers drifted toward us, and we strained to see them, our eyes streaming from the wind, noses running from the cold. The two ships came out of the clouds a long way off, like black wasps made sluggish by frost. They landed near the tree line, close enough to the power poles that the wires tossed in the rotor wash, and we boarded in twos, heads bent, breath caught in our throats as the downdrafts pounded our faces. There was a lot of hand rubbing and nose wiping after we had buckled in, and everyone turned to look through the open doors as we sailed back through the storm to our muddy camp. The forest stretched out below in a carpet of trees, the blackened patches, evergreens, and orange beetle-kill like a vast calico.

The storm turned to rain and killed what was left of the fire. We patrolled a few more times and found nothing, so the division supervisor placed us on standby, and we spent a week in camp with idle hands. Firefighters sign on to have fun and make money, so drawing eight hours a day—what we called straight eights—for playing cribbage or napping in a moldy tent tends to amplify any festering discontent in a crew, and we already had more than our share. If we'd continued to draw overtime for fieldwork, with daily helicopter rides, Jones would have swallowed his disgust for Claude, the rest of us would have kept mostly quiet, and we would have grumbled our way safely back home. But once we went on standby, our thrill seeking turned toward mutiny.

It is likely that the storms I have described were not as severe as they now seem because that week of standby acted as a powerful warp on our memory, aided by our need for memories of Claude's ineptitude. Jones was determined by now to call Lonna on one of the camp's remote phones, which we all knew would be a serious subversion of the chain of command. This was a moment of truth, a political moment, when crewmembers had to choose where they stood, like the moment in summer camp when you must decide whether you are in on pranking the weird kid in the corner bunk and, if not, how to avoid becoming a target yourself. I was on Jones' squad and I had been there when Lonna gave us her warning, so loyalty kept me from washing my hands of the plan to skewer Claude, though a certain schadenfreude also had me egging Jones on.

What was the case against Claude? The stories flourished over games of cribbage in the mess tent, where we spent most of our days on metal folding chairs whose legs sunk into the soggy ground. Between hands, we spit snoose into our paper coffee cups and rehearsed our memories, starting with the hailstorm and working backward. Flying a helicopter through hail is enough to get a pilot fired in the United States, and even if this decision owed something to the machismo of Canadian pilots, we were sure Claude had violated our safety policy by calling in the order. It must have been during this time that someone claimed to have witnessed a hotshot crew loading too much weight into one of the helicopters, so that when the ship tried to lift out of ground effect—the ballast gained from the rotor wash bouncing from the earth back up into the blades—the chopper began to nose-dive over the trees, banking so hard to get back to the landing strip in its free fall that it touched down off-center and bent one of its skids. Then the pilot just kicked one of the big guys out and lifted off again, as if such things were routine. This story gained so much traction among us that it now seems just as vivid and real to me as our flight out of Kalispell. It is only with discipline that I do not now tell the story as true, though all memory is a little like this, inextricable from the story one is telling about the present and as true as that self needs it to be.

———————

Jones got on the phone once we had our story straight and had a talk with Lonna, and then we quieted down for a few days, until some buzz started about an investigation. At that point Bill Gossage, the division supervisor, got involved. We had seen Bill around camp and should have gone to him first, which we surely would have done if our claims had been legitimate. Bill was a bearded old firefighter who seemed almost as lost as Claude. He mostly kept to himself in camp and ate alone in the mess hall, shoveling down huge platefuls of mashed potatoes and gravy. Like Claude, he had a hard time looking people in the eye, and so it was especially awkward when he started calling us one by one to his trailer office and asking us to verify the charges.

I went to see Bill on a pleasant afternoon, sunny and clear, near seventy degrees. He suggested that we meet outside, and so we sat beneath a pine tree behind his trailer. Bill leaned back on one elbow and fiddled with the pine needles, breaking them into little bits as he ran through his questions.

"I've got word from the forest supervisor back home that you all have some doubts about Claude," he said. "That's why I'm here, so I wish you'd all come to me from now on if you have concerns. But I do have to ask if Claude has done anything on this trip to make you feel unsafe." I ran through the stories we'd all been telling over cards, and Bill nodded. He'd heard it before. His face was sunken, as if he weren't sleeping well, and his eyes were bloodshot.

"OK, son," he said finally. "Thanks for your thoughts. You can go now." All twenty crew members went to Bill, and most of us had the same impression that he was just following orders, waiting out the last stretch of our three-week tour. We'd heard that our flight home would leave from Fort McMurray in a couple of days, so our bloodlust had worn off and we were mostly anxious to pile into the bus and leave the dirty camp. Tozzi made a softball by wrapping a small rock with several layers of duct tape, Jacobson whittled a bat from a green sapling, and we played a few pickup games bare-handed, stopping the hot grounders with our boots, dodging the gopher holes.

The day before we were to leave, Claude appeared near our row of tents and offered us a trip to Lac la Biche, which was at least forty miles away. He stood cockeyed, as usual, sighting down his lowered shoulder as he said there wouldn't be any more firefighting on this trip, so we may as well have a little fun.

"I don't mind if you have a beer or two," he said, "but just don't get out of hand."

The fact that Claude stayed behind should have struck us as odd, but we were so glad to get shut of that camp, even for an afternoon, we didn't stop to wonder. The bus groaned into gear, and then we were bumping through the hardened ruts, listening to Bauer heckle Jacobson with mock sorrow for leaving our little village. There was a steady murmur on the bus all the way to Lac la Biche like the happy rumble of talk at a church potluck, and when we pulled up to the Cheetah's Bar and Grill, everyone stood before the driver had stopped and ended up falling into the next seat when he hit the brakes. It was a mad scramble. Then we were wolfing down burgers and fries and draining pitchers of Molson as fast as the bartender could draw them.

A few of our party passed on Cheetah's and wandered down to the lakeshore. They might have seen the plaster-and-brick mosque that I later learned was one of the most famous landmarks in Lac la Biche. They would have seen loons on the lake and a few osprey, maybe a lone heron. They might also have seen that Claude had a purpose for sending us to town that they wanted to avoid. As inept a boss as he might have been, he was a schemer, and he surely knew that no crew of college kids who had been playing gopher ball and cards all week would be able to avoid growing unruly if they had a chance at beer.

He was right. It was a bleak trip back to camp. There were boozy skirmishes in the back seats, overturned spit bottles, and lots of pissing out the windows—a messy business on a bumpy dirt road. Claude was waiting for us when we returned, the bus headlights flashing against his glasses. He stood with his arms crossed while we filed out, and he might have been smiling as he surveyed the damage. We made our way to the tents in the chilly night, fell asleep in the dirt, and woke the next morning coated in grime.

———

Mutinous sailors either throw the captain overboard or hang for their crimes, but such fates are rare in the Forest Service. Lonna and the brass at the district office took a deposition from Claude after our return, where he presented time reports showing us on the clock during our binge in Lac la Biche. He claimed to have told us to lay off the booze, since we were on standby and could have been deployed to another fire at any time, even if our three-week tour was nearly up. His counterattack discredited us enough to kill the investigation into his safety violations. No one wanted to hear about our assumption that Claude had clocked us off for that afternoon, and while I felt outraged at the time, I don't blame them now.

Soon after Claude's deposition, Lonna tracked the four of us down, and Jones, Tozzi, Jacobson, and I went to see our fire management officer. Howard was a craggy man in his late fifties, half-deaf from running a chainsaw for too many years without earplugs. He had lost part of one lung, and his shortness of breath made him impatient with bullshit. When we protested that we weren't stupid enough to drink on the clock, he waved his hand.

"I don't give a good goddamn whether you were on the clock or not," he said. "You're supposed to be firefighters, for Christ's sake. That means being problem solvers, not troublemakers. We have enough clusterfucks without shit like this." Howard paused to cough, eyeing us from beneath his bushy eyebrows while he hacked into his hand. When he caught his breath, he licked his lips, glaring.

"Now, I've known you boys your whole lives. If I hadn't, I'd barbecue your asses right now. Even so, I should put a letter in your file. That's what the division supervisor wants me to do. But I know you're better than this, and I know you'll never do anything so goddamned stupid again, so I promised them this is the last horseshit they'll ever see from you. So, go on—get the hell out of here. Get back to work." We murmured our thanks as he waved us toward the door. Howard's tongue-lashing was a kind of pardon. We were punks but he forgave us. This instilled in me a great admiration for Howard, and aside from the shame I carried around for the rest of the summer, that was the end of it.

———

Fifteen years have passed. I have spun the Alberta tale over pints of Guinness, black coffee, and cold stream water. The story rises in my memory like smoke swirling above the original fire of that place and time. It is as if I am stumbling through the charred forest of my past, coated in ash as I search among the stump holes for a few embers to blow back into flame. Each time the coal bed ignites and the smoke pours forth, I kneel in the dust and watch the shape-changing faces unfold. I have remembered the trip to Alberta as a drama of near death by helicopter, a comedy of errors in the Forest Circus, and a lesson in staying uphill of one's own shit. Now, kneeling at the stump of this tale and fanning it alive again, I see a new story in the smoke.

The day after our lark in Lac la Biche, we all got drunk again, this time with Claude and Bill. We were staying at a hotel in Fort McMurray, planning to catch a flight back to Montana the next morning. That night we gathered in the cocktail lounge, a roomy space with a hardwood stage, a big-screen television, and at least a half dozen pink felt pool tables.

Like most beery memories, this one is hazy. But moments of clarity still surface in that state, when something seems so strange even drunk logic can't explain it, and for me such a moment came when Claude and Bill appeared at the bar.

For an hour or so we kept our distance, downing our pitchers at the pool tables, but soon Bauer was laughing with Claude while ordering another round, and then Pat Caspe was buying Bill a whiskey sour, and before long one of them convinced the bartender to power up the karaoke machine.

We each took a turn as the fool, following the bouncing ball while the others cheered, then we mobbed the stage and sang a string of traveling tunes—"Leavin' on a Jet Plane," "Jet Airliner," "Against the Wind." At two or three in the morning, after several last calls for booze, we badgered the bartender into one more song. Bill took the microphone for this one, and we all swayed like a choir behind him as he belted out "You've Lost That Lovin' Feelin'." I remember standing behind Bill as he crouched in anticipation of the chorus and swung his arm toward Claude, who was leaning against the bar, his spectacles like bright saucers of light above his gleaming cheeks, his hands clasped as if in triumph. That is how I have always remembered Claude. But I had one arm around Tozzi, the other around Jacobson, and the fog of youth in my head. I had no notion of how it might have felt to be clutching my own hand for solace, wishing to God I were home.

I spent the rest of the summer sharpening chainsaws and shovels and pulaski blades, tidying the tool cache, and waiting for one of the lookouts to call in a lightning strike. July came and went, and then it was August. My thoughts turned back to books, back to my other life, my migrations between Brigadoons. It was a rhythm I craved for the next ten years, a tango of escape and pursuit, the way partners move in the chase, each pivoting away and back and away again, only my partner changed faces. Sometimes I was chasing mountains and rivers and the life of the body, but every August I spun back toward Plato and Hawthorne and the heavy Tennessee nights, whirling around again in the spring toward streams booming with snowmelt and the promise of another fire season. With time I would settle down, learning to watch for renewal in the soil where I was also taking root. But for now it was a whirling dance every year—step, pivot, two-step—on into the future.

EIGHT

English Major

Around the time I flew back to Tennessee for my sophomore year, I saw a cartoon that summed up how I felt. It was a tetraptych, four portraits, of a young man, with a simple caption: "The Four Years of College." In the first he looked much as I did in my high school senior photo, clean-cut, serious, collar buttoned over a tie. In the sophomore portrait he had shoulder-length hair, a long beard, and hoop earrings, one hand raised in a peace sign. He mellowed somewhat as a junior, hair cropped to his ears but still falling into his face, the beard trimmed to a soul patch and goatee, the earrings now mere studs. And then his senior picture looked exactly like the first.

The cartoon has vanished, but I often think of it while speaking to first-year students who remind me of myself at that age, the ones with no doubts about their future plans. Mostly I let them talk and cheer them on. But there are always a few who sit a smidge too straight, who ruffle a little if I ask about a Plan B. Give yourself time, I say. You might not know yourself well enough yet to be quite so sure. These are the ones who come back as sophomores and ask: How did *you* choose your major? The short answer, I say, is that sometimes you don't choose your future. Sometimes it chooses you. The long answer takes me back to the smell of cotton, sunscreen, and clover, back to an immigrant girl watering a team of draft horses in Nebraska, her neck dark from the sun and her body lean and firm beneath her clothes.

My adviser, Dr. Snow, was a kindly man with a thick shock of gray hair and a gentle laugh, the lone Political Science professor at King College. He taught from a rickety lectern with an iron base and a wooden cabinet where he shuffled his coffee-stained notes after chalking an outline on the green blackboard. Beneath the desktop of the cabinet was a small shelf, about waist high, with just enough room for him to prop one knee as he spoke. It was a trick to keep our attention, like the gaps in his outlines that we were to fill as we jotted our notes, a moment we watched for every class, never quite sure when the right leg—always the right—would rise and slowly disappear into the lectern, until he stood before us like a great blue heron motionless in a bog. Once a joker asked Dr. Snow where he kept his leg for the entire period. He grinned and said, "In Narnia."

Dr. Snow oversaw the pre-law program, so I met with him every fall and spring in his office on the third floor of Bristol Hall, a crumbling brick building which also housed the History and English Departments. My law school ambitions were cooling fast after a few Political Science classes, where I found I could often rationalize at least two of the answers on the multiple-choice exams, almost always talking myself out of the correct one. I knew the questions were meant to prepare me for the Law School Admission Test, but the right answer often hinged on what felt like a petty distinction. No matter how fervently I challenged the questions I'd missed, Dr. Snow always smiled and insisted, politely, that I was wrong. At the start of my sophomore year, a crisis of confidence crept through my thoughts.

Why was I here? Scribbling notes on political action committees and the branches of government wasn't what I imagined while watching *Inherit the Wind* just two years ago. I could see no promontory of truth above the sea and fog, just a mess of fine print and nuances as void of life to me as one of Pluto's moons. Yet changing majors felt like quitting, so I kept scrawling notes the way I kept suiting up for baseball practice, where the ping of the aluminum bats left my ears ringing with futility.

At night I sought refuge with Ana, the Spanish teaching assistant from Uruguay. We met at a picnic table outside her dormitory where a sycamore stretched against the moon and the red dirt smell of the Appalachian hills rose from the ground. I'd light her cigarette and cup my hands around the fat end of my Camel Wide, the paper and tobacco crackling in the dark as the flame caught. A lamppost cast its light into the shadows, gleaming on our legs and arms and Ana's round face. Her hair hugged her cheeks like the petals of a tulip as she tossed her head back to laugh. We talked about God and art and sex while the cicadas roared, and I wondered if we'd ever be lovers. But Ana always had a boyfriend to complain about, some stubble-faced dude who wore a camouflage cap with the bill crunched into a half moon and a fishhook clipped to the side. The latest was Jack, an ex-Navy Seal, who I'd seen rattle off a set of thirty pull-ups in the college weight room. He was trouble, Ana said, but she couldn't make herself leave him. I drew hard on my cigarette and tried to look sympathetic.

I felt the opposite way about my major. It was slipping away, but I held on for fear of giving up. The men and women in my family knew how to hang tough. Once you found a job, you kept it for thirty, forty years. No whining, no hand-wringing about whether you might be happier elsewhere. God provided and you gave thanks and buckled down until God took the decision out of your hands again. Promises were so inviolable in my family that one of my cousins appeared at her fiancé's funeral—he'd been crushed by a tree on a logging job a few weeks before their ceremony—in her white wedding dress.

I needed an ironclad reason if I expected my change of heart to make sense to my father and the rest of my family. For most of them, books were for the long winter months when the firewood was split and stacked and snapping in the stove, when the family might gather for a portion of *The Hiding Place* or *The Cross and the Switchblade*. My mother ventured further as a young woman, persuading my father to purchase the Encyclopedia Britannica Great Books collection, hoping to educate herself from home. But most of the volumes still glistened in their shrink wrap, gleaming like another life just out of reach every time she ran a dust cloth down the shelf. I knew, though she never spoke of it, that my mother lived through me while I studied, dreaming her foregone past into our phone calls and letters.

A giant oak tree shaded my dorm room that year, a corner suite on baseball hall where I'd been assigned a new roommate. Calhoun was a North Carolina boy like Jackson, a tall, rangy kid with a similar penchant for clutter and dance parties and purple silk shirts. He kept his laundry in a fetid heap by his desk until he'd exhausted his supply of clean underwear and grew tired of going to class commando. I liked Cal and sometimes drove with him to a gas station in Bristol that had a beer tap by the soda machine where we could fill a gallon jug with Bud Ice and pass it off as apple juice if anyone got nosey back at the dorm. After we'd polished off our gallon, he'd talk about growing up with a single mother in Raleigh, how she sold pot to buy his school clothes, how he couldn't stand the stuff now. This was a big chance for him, coming to college, but I could tell he didn't expect to finish. An air of defeat soaked the room. I woke to it every morning in the shadow of the great oak, to the stench of the laundry pile, to Cal curled on his side, knees nearly tucked to his chin. And I carried it with me to Bristol Hall, where I copied more pages of notes to memorize, knowing even if I had the full notebook at my elbow for the next American Government exam, I might still miss the hair's breadth of reason on which the right answers turned.

The semester hunched along. Ana and I kept meeting beneath the sycamore tree, shivering in our jackets as October slipped into November. One night she shook her head when I offered a cigarette. Jack doesn't like it, she said, and I've been trying to cut back anyway. So I lit up and leaned back and listened to the latest about the joyrides on Jack's Harley and the time they snuck into the chapel and made love on top of the Steinway piano right in the middle of the stage. I'm so bad, Ana laughed. I smiled and blew a column of smoke into the night. *I'm right here*, I thought. *Right under your nose, whenever you want to wake up.*

It was nearly Halloween when I fell in love with another girl. I studied her in my American Literature class, drawn to the long dark hair falling into her face, the glow of her sun-darkened skin, her brown eyes wide and warm and full of light. She gazed at me from the cover of a novel, *My Ántonia*, the first book I'd ever read that spoke directly to my own family history. I recognized in Cather's sketches of immigrants arriving in Nebraska the faces of relatives I'd met during a family reunion at the Czech Days festival in Wilber, where my great-aunt Marcella told stories about my grandfather creeping between rows of onions on their farm during games of hide-and-seek. He was always the easiest to find, she said, because she could see the green onion tops waving as he pulled them to his mouth, munching the juicy shoots as he lay in the dirt. I knew how Jim Burden, the narrator, felt when he described the raw change of seasons in the country: "There was only—spring itself; the throb of it, the light restlessness, the vital essence of it everywhere: in the sky, in the swift clouds, in the pale sunshine, and in the warm, high wind—rising suddenly, sinking suddenly, impulsive and playful like a big puppy that pawed you and then lay down to be petted."

Against all this was Ántonia, the pretty peasant girl who coaxed a tiny cricket to sing in her cupped hands, who tried to cheer her father when the frontier broke his will, who gave up schooling to plow the cornfields with her brother and the farmhands. Even as a hired girl in town, Ántonia breathed with the vigor of the wild land, waltzing to the piano players who traveled through Black Hawk, sometimes inventing dances of her own as her feet beat the worn floorboards, her legs lithe and strong beneath her spinning dress. Cather brought me back to the summer mornings when my mother read to my sister and me on a quilt in the backyard beneath the plum tree, back to the afternoons I stole for myself in my bedroom, lying on the cold cement floor with *All Things Wise and Wonderful* as blissfully as Jim and Ántonia lay in the prairie grass with nothing but the blue sky and a golden tree to gaze upon. I'd meant to put these memories behind me as a young man, to fix my eyes on solid things, and most of the novels I had to read for class buttressed this goal. What could be more frivolous, I thought, than all the parlor talk, all the chatter between gentry trying to marry well. Even Melville seemed aloof to me then, his prose too littered with arcana to cast a lasting spell. And if I'd only been given James and Fitzgerald and Wharton to read, I'd surely have held stubbornly to my path, grinding away at a subject I did not love with no better reasons than work and career and hanging tough to prod me on.

But Cather coaxed blood and flesh from mere words. My people. My life. She took me to that place above the fog, the promontory where Whitman's spider cast his filament into the void, hoping it would catch hold somewhere. For my father this moment came in a garage, spotting a spelling gaffe on a Christian van, feeling certain this was proof he'd been chosen to spread the Good News. It was angelic tongues spilling from his mouth in an upstairs room at the Seattle commune. For my mother it was a bone memory of survival fanned aflame by revival meetings where the preachers raised their Bibles and cried, "Come get fresh bread!" It was bleeding to the very threshold of death then opening her Bible to a psalm that could serve as a guidepost if she ever neared that place again.

I let myself live between the pages of *My Ántonia*, where the shaggy prairie rolled beneath the wind like the memory of innocence, where the curtain between fact and fancy billowed and faded and then disappeared. I groaned when Ántonia was jilted by Donovan, the deadbeat railroad hand, who left her to raise their child in disgrace. I felt the sorrow of childhood friends parting and ached with Jim as he kept trying to come home even as his future dragged him away. My chest rose near the end as he got off the train in Hastings, Nebraska, driving a buggy out into the country-side to search for Ántonia's farm. When he found her and the wrinkles in her face fell away as he recognized the bright brown eyes of the girl he knew as a boy, I believed I could say with Jim: "I had the sense of coming home to myself."

One night I told Ana I was going to major in English. We were sitting at the picnic table, lamplight on our faces. "It's what I love," I said. "I can't fool myself any longer." She smiled. Shadows pooled in the hollows of her eyes as she sat with her arms crossed. She hadn't smoked in weeks.

"I have something to tell you, too," she said. "I'm pregnant." I felt my mouth turn dry.

"Jack doesn't want it. He thinks I should get an abortion, but I can't bear the thought." Tears rose in her eyes. "So I'm going home after finals. This time for good." I reached across the table for her hands, and then I walked to her side and took her in my arms. She wept softly against me. Leaves whispered in the sycamore tree. I closed my eyes and breathed her lilac perfume until we both rose, stiff with cold, to say goodnight.

When we said goodbye at Christmas, Ana made me promise to visit. "I'll be lonely, Juan," she said. "And you need to learn more *español*. I'll get you a teaching position." I kissed her cheek and gave my word.

———————

It was hard to go back to reading Hobbes and Locke after that, harder still to imagine four multiple-choice bullets on an American Government exam as the touchstones of my destiny, so that January I climbed the groaning stairs to the third floor of Bristol Hall and rapped on Dr. Snow's office door. He must have been napping, as he sometimes did before class, when he'd dash in at eight minutes past the hour just as we were packing our notebooks to leave. I heard a gasp and a loud thump after my knock, then the shuffle of his shoes over the carpet. When he opened the door and invited me in, turning to his desk, his magnificent gray hair bobbed in the back like a rooster's tail. I fiddled with my hands as I explained that I'd thought a lot about changing my major, hastening to add that it wasn't that I didn't enjoy his classes, I just wasn't sure law school would work out if I kept bungling the exams, and, anyway, I wanted to switch to English. Dr. Snow heard me out, his hands crossed in his lap.

"Why English?" he asked.

"I don't know," I said, feeling defensive. "Discussions feel more natural to me, and I'm better at writing than almost anything else." It was a weak answer, I knew, a kind of waffling I normally disdained. Was I really trading law school for *discussions*? My father would not be pleased.

Dr. Snow considered that and leaned over his desk. "So we're done with pre-law, then? What do you think you might do with an English major?"

"Maybe journalism," I said. "Maybe grad school. Maybe I'd want to teach. I guess I need to think it through." What I knew, but could not yet express, was that everyone needs a story to live by, and I thought I'd found mine. It was a flash of recognition I'd been watching for all my life, the sense that Cather revealed me to myself, breathing a mythic power into my past that I'd never fully glimpsed, like the plough Jim and Ántonia saw one evening against the setting sun, the black blade magnified for an instant within the burning orb before falling back into the prairie dusk.

In a few years I'd follow that feeling to Nebraska for graduate school, traveling with my Cather seminar to Red Cloud, where I saw the home of Annie Pavelka, Cather's childhood friend and prototype for Ántonia, and met Annie's granddaughter, Antonette, a chatty Czech woman who had lived the novel for so many years that she spoke of the character and her grandmother as one. Our professor, who insisted we call her Sue, walked us through the old opera house, the railroad depot, Cather's childhood home, showing how faithful the novels we'd been reading were to this real place, and I saw that the little town, so much like my native Troy, was now forever lit up by its past. After reading *O Pioneers!* and *The Song of the Lark*, I knew that beyond the chipped Sinclair sign, down the weedy alley behind the old Baptist church, there were still people like Alexandra Bergson and Thea Kronborg waiting to be seen for who they half-knew themselves to be, that this could be true of any place. And at the end of the day, when Sue drove us south of town to a patch of virgin prairie just large enough to lie down in and imagine the wild land before it began shearing away from the plough, I felt a deep gratitude to Cather for helping me see more here than a vacant pasture.

That day in Red Cloud was still a few years away when I shook Dr. Snow's hand and creaked down the stairs in Bristol Hall as an English major. It was a relief to let law school go, to unclench that pretense. I stepped out into the chilly afternoon and lit a cigarette as I walked back to the dorm. The term was nearly finished. After flying back to Montana in May for another summer with the fire crew, I'd need a good story when my father sat me down to explain—I'd edit the school paper, maybe intern with a magazine, check out some master's programs. I was still working it out as I snuffed my Camel on the brick wall of the dorm.

It was nearly dinnertime. Laughter and the chirp of a Super Mario Brothers game ricocheted down the hall, the thump of stereo bass buzzing the light fixture overhead as I walked to my corner room. The reek of Cal's clothes rose when the door swung open, and I shot the dirty heap with a cloud of Lysol before I sat down at my desk. I opened *My Ántonia* and read the last chapter again: Jim's goodbye to Ántonia after their reunion, passing the wagon ruts from the pioneer road that had been cut deeper by rain, like the marks of a bear's claws slashed into the plains, the wheels of fate and fortune and accident that brought Ántonia to Jim, then drew him away, and finally carried him back to her. I thought about what it meant to come home to myself.

Then I saw there was an appendix that we'd not been assigned, Cather's original introduction to the novel. It was mostly the same as the one we'd read for class, an unnamed narrator happening upon Jim Burden, a childhood friend, as the two rode a train across the Iowa plains through crushing summer heat, reminiscing about their hometown. The revised introduction ended with another reunion in New York, when Jim brought his friend a sheaf of pages he'd written, everything he could recall about Ántonia. It was a clever way to frame the narrative, drawing attention away from Cather and easing into Jim's first-person point of view. But the original introduction ended a little differently. Before Jim gave his version of Ántonia's story to his unnamed friend, whom I now imagined as myself, he asked, "Now, what about yours?" I looked up from my desk out the dorm window, where the oak's branches swayed on a breeze, and then the oak was a plum tree, and I lay in its shade on a quilt with my sister, a book open between us as we listened to our mother read.

NINE

Uruguay

It was a slow descent into Montevideo, zooming in on neighborhoods sprawled beneath the *paraíso* and *olmo* trees. As I turned away from the window, my neighbor's face beamed over my shoulder. "*¿Muy tranquilo, no?*" I nodded and smiled, but I had already forgotten the scene below. After a mind-numbing series of flight connections from Seattle to Buenos Aires, I wanted nothing more than to drop my suitcase somewhere I could call home for the next year. Now the plane was touching down, rocking from one wheel to the other as the cabin shook. I raised a silent prayer.

The plan was to stay with Ana's mother. We had been talking about this since Ana left college, when I had promised her I would visit. Four years had passed, and I was twenty-three years old, a newly minted MA brimming with wanderlust. All of my friends were marching into doctoral programs, so far as I could tell because they could no longer imagine anything else. I longed to take more courses with my mentor, Sue, a leading Cather scholar who also taught environmental literature. But the stories I'd heard from PhDs graduating that year who applied for a hundred jobs and maybe, if they were lucky, secured two interviews, convinced me that I needed to know in my very marrow what I wanted before embracing the profession.

Ana and I kept in touch all this time, and when I decided to take a year or two to think things through, she was quick to invite me to Uruguay. "When will you get another chance?" she wrote. "You'll see, it will be good for you. Everyone is so *amable* here. I know you'll feel right at home." When I thought of Ana I felt a visceral tug like I had when I heard flamenco music for the first time and wanted to eat those beefy chords.

And why not give teaching a try, to see if I had the right stuff? Ana taught at St. Catherine's School, a bilingual *colegio* in Minas, and she knew of an opening for the sixth grade, a full-time position that she said would give me enough cash for weekend travel. Twenty hours of face time a week, she said, with all of your mornings free for prep and grading. As a native English speaker with a master's degree, I wouldn't need any other certification. It sounded perfect. I told her to sign me up. The important thing was I would get to hold her again—at least one big hug to say hello. I lost myself in memories of Tennessee throughout the flight. I could almost smell the lilac perfume she wore.

My head was thick with fatigue when I stepped from the plane in Montevideo into the humid air. I remember the walk from customs to the baggage claim as a dark Monet—heat waves on the tarmac, blurry queues stretching back from the booths, three wide windows smeared by handprints. Once inside I searched the crowd for Ana. A frantic hand caught my eye. I followed it to the unfamiliar face of a blond woman in midlife, eyebrows raised, mouth wide in a false smile. She waved harder when our eyes met, so I hitched her way, suitcase banging against my leg.

"I am Rosa," she gushed.

The quiet man at her side extended a broad palm. "*Soy Francisco. Papá de Ana.*"

I grinned and gripped his hand. "*Mucho gusto.* Nice to meet you."

"Sorry about Ana," Rosa said, as if I already knew.

———————

It was an hour's drive from Montevideo to Minas, where Ana lived near her family. Francisco drove silently, one hand dangling from the wheel. Furrows crisscrossed his dark face. A crucifix swung from the mirror. Rosa twisted around in her seat, and I could see Ana's features in hers, the same round cheeks and brown eyes. "*¿Ana está bien?*" I asked. Rosa forced a smile. "*No te preocupes,*" she said. "Don't worry."

It was December, summer in the southern hemisphere. Sheep milled about on the brown hillsides. Eucalyptus groves flashed past in a shifting matrix of trees. Occasionally, if I watched closely, those long corridors would give me a split-second glimpse into the distance. To pass the time I fell into a daydream from my youth, imagining a giant blade running perpendicular to the car, lopping off the telephone poles and fence posts, slicing through everything that fell across my line of sight.

Rosa's house in Minas shared walls with a candy store and a neighboring home. She was a lawyer, and it said so on her door—Rosa García, Abogada—engraved on a brass plate. After Francisco and Rosa helped me unload my things, I leaned against the car to hide the sweat on the backs of my thighs. The air smelled of burnt rubber. The front door swung open, and a little boy, no more than a toddler, ran out onto the sidewalk. He was followed by a thin young man in a white T-shirt and faded jeans who wandered up to me, flipped a shock of blond hair out of his face, and stuck out his hand.

"Hey. Ah'm Chris." His clammy fingers folded together in my grip. Over his shoulder I could see the boy looking back through the open door. Ana's eyes were lowered when she stepped out, dozens of pounds thinner than when I had seen her last. Black slacks matched the hollows in her cheeks. She took the little boy's hand. "*Hola Juan,*" she said.

The next afternoon I found Ana alone at the kitchen table. Her son played in the courtyard, his laughter drifting through the window screen. I would never have recognized her on the street. Her skin was ashen, her eyes puffy. She sat with her elbows on the table and her head thrown back a little, the way she used to look when she laughed. But there were no curves in her cheeks now, just angles and shadows. She blew a straight stream of smoke toward the ceiling as I sat down, then immediately drew hard on the cigarette. I had not smoked since I saw her last, but there was a pack lying open on the table, so I lit one up.

"*¿Como estás, Ana?*" Smoke trickled out of her nostrils as she looked toward the courtyard without answering.

"You don't have to tell me anything. But I don't know why this guy Chris is here. I don't know what's going on with you."

She laughed without smiling. "He thinks we're in love. I don't know how to make him go home. *Estoy enferma, Juan.*"

The next day she admitted herself to the local asylum for manic depression. Francisco took her. They went quietly while I was asleep in the courtyard, a book forgotten in my lap.

I lay awake that night and the next. I had nearly decided to bag the whole plan. Then Rosa came home from the hospital with two notes written in an unsteady hand. Chris showed me his note. It read, "I'm sorry, you should go. This is a bad time." He asked about my note, but I did not show it to him. It said, "Don't leave, Juan. I need you here."

———————

After Chris left I moved to Ana's apartment for a couple of weeks. The lease would run out at the end of December, and I planned to move back in with Rosa then. This would buy the family some time alone. Ana had begun electroshock treatments, and her parents were the only visitors allowed. I was not sure I could really help, but I desperately wanted to see Ana again, so I moved into her flat.

Ana lived on the second story of a cement building near the town square. When I turned the key and nudged the door open with my knee, the smell of cumin and chili powder rose with the draft. Toy cars lay scattered over the floor, a purple sweater hanging from a chair as if she might come back at any moment. I inched sideways through the kitchen with my guitar and suitcase, my backpack brushing along the counter. A Spanish arch led to the hallway, to the bedroom and bath.

Compared to the rest of the flat, Ana's room seemed enormous. I shut the *armario* to avoid looking at her clothes hanging there and tossed my backpack onto the bed. A sliding glass door led to the balcony overlooking the street. 18 de Julio was a thoroughfare named for the day Uruguay accepted its constitution, one wide lane of traffic buzzing through the city center at all hours. I leaned for a moment on the railing, surveying the *frutería* across the way before stepping back inside to sit on the rumpled bed, where the comforter still held the shape of a woman's hip.

Each morning I descended the stairs to buy bread from the *panadería* two doors down. A kiosk around the corner sold canned tuna. Aside from the occasional *chorizo al pan* from street vendors, these were my meals.

Nights, I sat on the balcony above 18 de Julio until the drone of the street weighed heavily on my eyes. Then the dark house, the bedroom door looming overhead, and finally the bed, still smelling of lilac. Rattling walls as I drifted off.

Every night I had the same dream. It came in different forms—strangulation, heart attack, burial under intolerable weight—but it always began and ended the same way. A moped with no muffler would turn onto

18 de Julio about a quarter mile in the distance at a quiet hour. About that time I was usually somewhere in subconscious bliss, camped in the Rocky Mountains, lying in Nebraska grass, listening to cicadas while I smoked in Tennessee. Wherever I was in my dream, a pall crept over the landscape when the bike started to go through the gears. Dread swelled in my chest, my body twisting toward a threshold that broke when the engine ripped past on the street.

I thought I loved Ana, and this surely kept me in Minas. But something larger was at stake. When others around me had fallen apart, I had persevered. My mother attributed this to a spiritual covering, which she believed protected the family from harm, some blood sign upon our door that kept the plagues at bay. Such knowledge was to carry us through the unknown without injury, and so far that had held true for me. But it was a tortured logic that buoyed my sense of self, the mountaintop feeling that I could always rise above trouble. More than anything else this belief held me in Uruguay. I could not leave without keeping my promise, because I had not yet learned how to break an oath before it broke me.

Knowing what I do now about mental illness, Ana's note from the hospital could not have signified trust, at least not in the way I perceived it then. Nor was it guile, though that was how it felt later on. She was grasping for a handhold on a crumbling bank, the roar of despair in her ears. Unlike me, she was able to ask for help.

Soon after Ana left, when the severity of her illness had become clear, I met with Lupe, the director of St. Catherine's School. Lupe was a plumpish woman in her late fifties. She had short dark hair and an imperious air, lifting her chin as she spoke. Lupe asked me to take on Ana's high school courses in addition to the full-time contract I'd signed for the sixth grade. It would mean adding twenty-six contact hours, a full five hours every morning from the opening bell to lunch, and I protested that it felt like too much to shoulder with no real teaching experience. Lupe shrugged her mouth. It will be easy, she said. Literature and history, right up your alley. We need another native English speaker, and with your credentials you'll have no trouble. You know this stuff—all you have to do is get up and talk. I felt a weariness creeping over me as she waved my objections away, and finally I said, sure, I'll do it for Ana's sake. Whatever I can do to help.

But in the following weeks, as I brooded alone at the flat, reality began to sink in. The lease had nearly expired. Fretting about it wouldn't keep the landlord away. Rosa and Francisco were preoccupied with visits to the hospital and caring for Ana's son. The last thing I wanted was to impose further on them, yet I would soon be homeless. If Lupe wanted me to take on Ana's classes, I thought, if I was bailing the school out of that jam, then surely I was within my rights to ask for housing. One afternoon I picked up the phone.

Lupe was not pleased to hear from me. When she answered her cell, I could hear surf breaking nearby.

"I'm on vacation," she said. "Can't this wait?"

"Look," I said. "The lease is almost up. Rosa can't take me in again, so I need to find a place to stay. Could the school sign a new lease?"

"No way, we're not going to pay that kind of rent." The receiver crackled as she shouted to her grandchildren. "*¡Chiquilines! ¡Cuidado!*"

My eyes burned. I tried to steady my voice. "Well, I don't know what you want me to do. Ana is getting shock treatments and I can't see her and you've asked me to take a double teaching load, which I'm glad to do, but I've got to find someplace to stay by the end of the week."

She fell silent for a moment. Through the phone I could hear the breakers and the babble of children at play. Her breath came over the line in nasal gusts. I imagined her in a sunbonnet there on the beach, picnic basket and cooler nearby, ice-cream vendor within earshot. My thoughts were not kind.

"Fine," she said. "Let me see what I can do."

———

The next morning I sat reading on the balcony. When the buzzer rang I leaned over the railing to see who it was. A balding man looked back, sweat stains blotching his polo shirt.

"*Hola,*" I said. "*¿Quién es?*"

"Raúl—friend of Ana." I let him in and he climbed the stairs, wheezing a little as he went. He would not sit when I offered a chair. His hair was thin, but his wide chin and thick forearms suggested lingering strength.

"I need few things," he said. "Ana live with me when she get out." My lips made the shape of a smile as I followed him into the kitchen. The refrigerator went first, then the range. I helped him maneuver both down the stairs. They fit neatly into the back of his Toyota pickup. He drove away without a word, returning an hour later. This time the couch and table went. Finally we packed her clothes and the remaining groceries into his front seat. Only the bed remained, but he did not hesitate. He yanked the sheets off, tossing them over the balcony railing into his truck. After finessing the mattress around the corners in the stairwell, we disassembled the frame and were done. He offered his hand. *"Que pase bien,"* he said. Have a good one.

I trudged back up the stairs and walked from room to room, taking in the bare walls and empty floor. My suitcase stood where the couch had been. That night I spread a towel on the floor and folded a dirty shirt under my head, smashing ants on my arm until sleep overtook me.

At a quiet time of night after I'd drifted off, a moped with no muffler turned onto 18 de Julio and ground through all the gears. I was dreaming of the ocean, bobbing chest-high in the waves, when the drone cast its pall over the scene. Then there was no bottom as I was sucked and spun into the depths. The water moaned as I gasped for air. Just before my chest burst, the scooter screamed by on the street, and I sat up with a ragged breath to face the empty wall.

———

After Raúl gutted the flat, I hit a low point. Ana's note sat on the floor, rumpled and smudged from the times I'd reread it to assure myself that she wanted me to stay. If I could have seen her, we would have fallen into the old roles of confessor and confidant, and I would have had the usual messianic reason for sticking around. As it stood, I could not yet admit to myself that my purpose was to shoulder her teaching load, freeing her from obligations to the school and clearing the way for her new life with Raúl. The implications were too insulting to contemplate. What would it mean if I was not the one taking her into my arms—if, instead, I was being taken in? Beneath the paranoia was a deeper fear about the truth of prayers and their power to cover me, a sense that maybe trouble could touch me after all.

I haunted the Internet cafes, trying to get my bearings by writing to family and friends. I plied them all with questions. Some thought I should go. The most devout were certain that good would come of it all. Remember Romans 8:28, they said: "And we know that all things work together for good to them that love God, to them who are called according to his purpose." My father was resolute in encouraging me to stay. He was fond of analogies, though they were often bizarre. He wrote: "I was just thinking of Corrie Ten Boom and how she managed to love her persecutors even in the concentration camps." St. Catherine's School was no Auschwitz, but my father's comparison characterized the inflated self I was trying to inhabit. All of the arrows pointed toward my narrative of promise, my indestructible faith. The truth is I did not stay in Minas to help Ana, nor did I stay there because I cared about teaching, at least not initially. After meeting Raúl, I stayed to protect my narrative of self. Soon enough I would learn that experience is the touchstone for self making, that even the most essential certainties can fall away.

———————

The Hotel Verdún was my new home. The hotel was very white. It sat on a corner of the town square across the street from a prison yard. The cramped foyer opened into a lounge lit by a high glass ceiling, where cane trees and palm plants sprouted from the ceramic pots lining the walls and a clutch of armchairs circled a stone hearth. The arrangement came about because the owners, whose children attended St. Catherine's, were behind on their tuition payments. I did not want to imagine their conversation with Lupe. It left a chill. Marcos was always smiling at the front desk. "¿Andas bien, Juan?" But beneath the smiles we both knew I had come by force.

The room was quiet, tucked well away from the street—two beds, a closet, and a bath. The lone window opened over the courtyard, little more than clay tile and a central shrub ringed by whitewashed walls. I had room enough for my clothes in the closet, and the top shelf held my suitcase. My books and paper went to the extra bed. I lay down to take it all in, and for a few moments I sighed with relief. Then a pang of loneliness struck. I longed to be with Ana, and the memory of lugging furniture out of the flat with her aging lover came back like a desert wind. Pinpricks of heat broke out over my forehead and neck.

Why not leave? It seems an obvious question now. But by then I had begun to justify my decision. It was too near the start of the school term. I had shouldered forty-six hours of classes—twenty from before and twenty-six of Ana's high school credits. Surely they could not find someone to replace them all, and I did not want to be the person who left all that to someone else. They were counting on me. It was a way to prove I could still reach higher ground.

St. Catherine's School owned two stone buildings in Minas within a block of each other: one for the high school (*liceo*) and the other for grades one through six (*primaria*). Each had large wooden doors so caked with green paint they were soft to the touch. The doors were eight feet tall, bolted to the stone walls with iron ties like the entrance to a church. Like most Uruguayan institutions, St. Catherine's retained only nominal Catholic ties, waiving classes in catechism and ignoring most feast days. The school was as different from Catherine of Siena, its self-mutilating namesake, as it could be. Twice a year Lupe dropped in from the headquarters in Montevideo to scold, cajole, and admonish the cadre, but mostly the school ran as it pleased.

As a first-time teacher I struggled to find my bearings. When my colleagues met a week before the first day of classes to plan for the upcoming term, I expected to see lesson plans, assignments, and calendars. Instead I received a stack of books. The other teachers were pleasant, but I internalized my doubts. *What do I do when the lesson is finished too early? How do I get through four hours every afternoon with a pack of wild kids?* Such questions seemed too foolish to ask. They could only be answered by doing.

This is the story of any rookie: the self-doubt, the numbness before leaping into the fray. And from my vantage now, none of these anxieties needed to have meant half as much as they did. But I had traveled too far from myself to recover, like a skier who has fallen midway on a difficult run and must finish the descent. This was difficult to communicate to others, because even while I was retreating into denial about the sheer magnitude of my duties, I was overwhelmed by the reality of my solitude. Still, there was a certainty in loneliness. It was something I could choose.

Despite my inwardness, one teacher befriended me. Claudia was a tall Italian woman with piercing eyes and a runner's build. Her son Nacho would be in my class, so it was surely motherly concern that sparked her interest, but we soon grew close in my platonic way.

By the time classes had begun, my double life was well established. The public face remained impassive. *No problem. I've got it covered.* The private face was a montage of trouble. I knew my mother found a refuge in prayer, weathering many trying times on her knees. Disciplined silence, I thought, should quiet the heart enough to hear the still, small voice of God. But for me prayer was no more than a daydream, a scatter of thoughts. My most earnest petitions were short bursts of panic. *Get me out of this. Keep me alive. Let it work out OK.* This is not enough when the self is slipping away. The self needs firmer footing. And so, after many weeks of paralyzing doubts, I turned to rituals of the body, which had always made more sense to me. I began eating nothing but bread and fruit. And I began to run.

———

Despite all of the sympathetic clucking I had heard from my primary school colleagues about the sixth-grade class I was to take over—reputedly the worst behaved in the history of the school—they were meek on the first day. There were eight. Nacho was a handsome boy with dark hair and an athlete's face. His eyes drank up the room. Inés was his closest friend. I remember the flash of her smile and her stories about dreams where she and Nacho battled lions and giant snakes. Lucía was blond with brown eyes. She was the shortest in the class but had no trouble shoving her way through the crowd at recess. Sebastian was a troublemaker. I could tell this from his bucktoothed grin and cowlick and from the fact that scarcely two minutes into the introductions on the first day he had already kicked Inés under the table. There were two Santiagos, each known by his surname. Effinger was a man-child, beefy and troubled, nearly six feet tall. Gadea was a petite boy with straight black hair, a nervous laugh, and the neatest penmanship in the class. Martín had a dark, smooth face and was nearly as tall as Effinger. Then there was Gonzalo, a small boy, given to sudden out-bursts and brooding silence.

We met each afternoon in a room with eight green desks facing each other and scarcely enough space for me to slide along the plaster wall behind the chairs. A chalkboard hung at the front of the room near a small table that served as the teacher's desk. Posters spangled the walls: rainforest birds, a smiling indigenous child, the Apollo 17 Earth photo. Through the wooden doors to my left, as I stood at the front of the class, was the school's entryway. This corridor emptied into a common area with a checkered tile floor. A piano sat against the wall, and a corner door led to the reading room. Straight ahead was the cobbled playground, where I could release my delirious children once a day, stand like a sentinel, and chat with Claudia for a few moments before herding them back. Most of my memories of St. Catherine's begin in that musty classroom, as if I slept and woke there.

In truth my days began well before dawn. I had never taught before, so I was dashing blindly through this routine, planning a dozen different lessons in the predawn hours, papers strewn over the spare bed, then hotfooting it through the town square to my 7:30 class at the *liceo*, where I taught until noon. An hour later I began my afternoon shift at the primary school and soldiered through until 5:00. Then my daily run, dinner, and grading until bed. I had no time for memories and even less for sadness, though it was always there, that buried yearning. I dared not think of it, lest the toothpick fortress of my routine give way. And so it was that I turned to my ascetic ways.

Uruguayan bread is made of white flour, and it took me some time to realize that I could request a loaf of whole wheat at the local *panaderías* (*Pan negro, por favor*). The bread came in three conjoined sections. For lunch I broke off a third and ate it like the Eucharist. A handful of bread, an apple, a bottle of water. One cornerstone of my day. One decision I no longer had to make. Dinner was the rest of the loaf and an orange. An indiscriminate eater, I relished variety and often overindulged. But this was not about pleasure. It was about sticking to the plan. Over time, two sections of the loaf felt like an extravagance. Then the orange. (What decadence.) I was learning to understand a few baked grains, learning to live in the space between mouthfuls, feeling the flesh as the one true thing.

After the honeymoon of the first day, the sixth-grade class reverted to its usual ways. Sebastian was always the center of the ruckus, a pinching, spitting, face-making dervish. Effinger labored so long over his work that the others would grow impatient and pelt him with spitballs if my back was turned. Such things happened so often I can only recall them in the plural, like a time-lapse photo. Always Sebastian's leering face—cowlick, ears, toothy grin—Effinger's cheeks reddening, then his rumbling shout, *¡Dejate de joder!* Stop messing with me! Gadea tittering. Nacho turning from his reading, and Inés catching his eye. Martín blushing as he laughed. Gonzalo looking on, bemused.

It was not a happy chaos. Once I went blind with anger, the room darkening as I shouted for order. Another time, as the din intensified, my voice rising with the rest, Lucía stood on her chair and let loose a scream. Bedlam. For self-preservation I learned to deflect noise with silence. Gentle answers did not turn away all wrath, but they kept me together until I laced up my running shoes.

—————

Running began as self-torture, much like my high school weightlifting routine. My legs were geared for strength, not speed. But I hungered after pain. It was something real. Those burning lungs, the feverish weakness in my bowels, the aching shins—they were my refuge from thoughts of Ana, the way I sought to strip myself of memory.

The dirt path began on the edge of town. To get there I walked from the hotel through several blocks of graffiti-sprayed gates, and homes made of cement blocks. At the edge of the barrio I crossed a yellow bridge, glancing down at the river, which rose and fell with the rain. During the dry spells, plastic bags festooned the overhanging brush.

Across the bridge, where the highway led out into the countryside, I began my stretches on the grassy shoulder. A few toe touches and lunges, then some seated poses, and I'd begin, crunching through gravel up the first hill, legs and chest tightening. A little reprieve at the top. Blue sky overhead, smell of eucalyptus trees. Slow strides over a long flat, starting to labor again. Head bent to the ground. Cars buzzing on the highway. Then a big hill, gunning toward the top, eyes blind, one column of flame from heel to throat. I took a turn at the crest, near the green 6k marker, then eased into the descent, cool air flooding my chest. Back on the flat, I quickened my pace, seeing nothing but the grassy mat underfoot and the ruts baked hard into the path. Gliding over the first hill, I sprinted all out back to the bridge, belly boiling, chest enraged.

Most days I lingered at the trail's end, hands on my knees, thoughts gone to fog. Then the slow walk back to the hotel through the barrio, along the prison fence to the white arches of Verdún. Marcos at the front desk. "¿Todo bien, Juan?" The cold shower. Bread and orange. Back to the papers strewn over the spare bed.

———————

It is difficult to pull places and times from those first few months. What I remember best are patterns and rituals. My high school students were well behaved, so most of my mornings, even while teaching, were spent thinking anxiously about my afternoon class. I pushed a pseudoself through those early hours. Small things jarred me out of distraction. A curvy senior, Paola, struggled with English and often came to my desk for help, brushing my shoulder with her breast. Two identical twins, Franco and Marco, sat at opposite sides of the room like a magic trick, the same Roman face wherever I turned. But memory has a way of sanitizing itself. My high school students allowed me to withdraw, so my thoughts of them cannot be trusted. We would have to meet again.

More and more the sixth-grade class drove me to desperation. I was the son of necessity during those months, grasping after anything to keep them engaged. My greatest triumph was a vocabulary drill that killed at least an hour each day. American newspapers are said to be written for comprehension at the sixth-grade level, so I gathered as many online articles as I could, made copies, and doled them out each week. The class was to read each article aloud, circling words they did not understand. Cocky. Legislate. Acute. Vernacular. Surreptitious. I asked each student to write a word on a small card, look up the definition, and then illustrate the card, using markers and crayons to give the word a personality that would match its definition. I found a wall hanging made from a sheet of blue fabric, with plastic pockets for the letters of the alphabet, and we began alphabetizing the words.

After a few weeks we had a sizable cache of new vocabulary, so I began many classes by dividing the group into pairs least likely to disintegrate into eye scratching and yelling. Each pair chose five words from the vocabulary bank and integrated them into an imaginary dialogue. Sometimes we brainstormed scenarios. *A man is on a park bench contemplating suicide—convince him to live. You are saying goodbye to your best friend, who is moving to another country. A knight confronts a sorcerer who is about to curse a city.* Time to choose the words. Time to compose the dialogue. Time to perform each sketch. For an hour each day my cramped room was filled with murmuring children lost in thought, tongues pressed between their lips as their pencils scratched over the paper. Then the other three hours began.

It was as if we were on a road trip, all eight children crammed into the back seat. My heart raced when I saw the sidelong glances and the kicks under the table, because I knew the immortal spitball was close behind, then snot wiped on a neighbor's sleeve, the mouthed obscenities. *Maricón. Imbécil. Tu madre trabaja en la esquina.* I knew all was lost when the animal noises began. *Mooooo*, one student would say. *Ar-ar-ar-ar*, cried another. *Caaawww, caaawww*, another would crow as the blood rose in my eyes.

Twice a week we walked down the hall, over the checkered tiles of the common room, and into the library. White bookshelves lined the walls, beanbags and quilts strewn over the floor. Reading time was thirty minutes. Each student was to choose a book, find a place to sit, and keep quiet. The plan might have worked had it not been for Sebastian, who peered over the top of his book until he caught a classmate's eye. If I asked him to turn his back, he sighed and shuffled his feet on the carpet. Once I gripped him by the shoulder and led him out into the common room, his cowlick bobbing as we walked, his buckteeth pressed into his lower lip in the usual smirk. When I pointed at the floor, he slouched against the stone wall and pretended to read. I returned to the others and had nearly quieted them when Effinger let out his goofy laugh and pointed toward the windowed door. Sebastian had flattened his nose and tongue against the glass, his eyes crossed and both hands waving from his ears. I longed for a good stiff cane.

But this was a progressive school, and I used the full range of non-violent discipline. Some days I withheld recess. If that failed, I'd assign handwritten copies from the history textbook. Trips to the principal's office were next, then phone calls to parents. I wrote each student's initials on the board and kept track of demerits. Three demerits meant no recess. Five meant no recess and one page copied longhand from the history book. Six meant no recess, one page copied during recess, two pages to copy for homework. When the novelty of this system wore off, I tallied demerits for half the day, then rewarded good behavior after recess by taking demerits away. But this was a group identity I could not crack. They might be tricked into learning for an hour or two, but they soon recovered their real purpose, which was to drive me mad. My class had seen the other teachers shaking their heads for six years. Most of the eight students had emerged unscathed from parent-teacher interventions. They knew their power. Time was on their side. They would wear me down.

It was late afternoon on a rainy day. I had taken the class to the *liceo* for a research assignment on the computers. The room was dark. Stools scraped over the tile floor as students settled into their pairs. The assignment was to find three of Galileo's discoveries by searching the Internet. I planned to use these findings for a composition the next day, but as usual there were more immediate concerns than the lesson. In the space of five minutes, Gonzalo had opened an online game of Asteroids, mimicking the sound as he fired each shot. *Pkew, pkew.* Sebastian was pinching Gadea. *Ahhhh.* *¡Basta!* Lucía and Inés were engrossed with glamour shots of Shakira. It was a mass mutiny. As soon as I had coached one pair back on task, the others had run amok. I had no new threats to give and searched myself in vain for new rewards. Even Nacho and Martín, two students I could usually count on, were laughing. "I can't help it, teacher," Nacho said. "It's a *fracaso*." At that moment Gadea yelled again in pain, and before I could think I had Sebastian by the ear, lifting him from his stool and jerking him across the room—*owww, owww*—where I threw him against the wall, stuck my finger in his face, and hissed, "I've had enough of your crap for a lifetime."

His face crumpled. The others fell silent as he sobbed. I got them turned around, completed the assignment, and then herded the somber bunch back to our room in time for the final bell. As the children were filing out, I was dialing Sebastian's mother. She was unhappy, but she understood. She'd heard it before. While the other teachers exulted in the story, glad the little *pica* got what was coming to him, it haunted me. Something was changing. I was turning mean. The bread-and-fruit ceremony wasn't working, nor was the running. The sheer crush of work had forced me to live in the nutshell of the present for many weeks, but now the denial was fading. Memories were coming back. Tennessee. "Don't leave, Juan." Raúl. *"Que pase bien."* It was April, and I had already begun counting the days until December, when my contract with St. Catherine's would expire. Doubts were creeping in.

———————

I had not allowed myself to contemplate leaving once classes began. It would have been one thing to cut and run before the start of a job, but I had been raised to finish what I started. There were no more illusions about helping Ana. Rumors trickled through St. Catherine's about her sugar daddy and the high life they were living in Punta del Este—the shopping sprees and the bungalow on the beach. My only purpose now was to survive the year. I had been drifting through each morning, measuring mouthfuls of bread at midday, grasping after any stalling tactic to get through the four interminable afternoon hours, then punishing myself on the earthen path each night. There was order here, but I did not like the shape it was taking. When I cut the lamp in my hotel room and looked over the empty courtyard, moonlight glowing on the whitewashed paling, my window could have been the mouth of a sepulcher.

One night after dinner at Claudia's house, I sat in her car outside the Hotel Verdún. The moon beat against the prison wall. The hotel gleamed across the street. Claudia lit a cigarette, its red eye glowing in the shadowed cab. I felt a bubble expanding in my chest.

"What if I were to leave in July?" My belly washed cold with the thought. "Eh?"

"What would happen if I quit at the end of the quarter?"

"Nothing would happen. Lupe would find another teacher, *y ya*. They're all surprised you're still here. What are you afraid of?" Her cheeks hollowed as she drew on the cigarette.

"I don't know. I guess I thought there might be trouble with *Migración*, since I signed a contract with St. Catherine's."

"*Migración* won't care. If you need to go, then go."

Pressure built in my chest. My throat ached. I watched a large moth bump into the windshield, folding its spotted wings as it came to rest. "It's impossible," I said. "Even with half the teaching load, more time to travel . . . It's just that I've killed myself trying. And I don't know how all this happened with Ana, how she could change so much. Why couldn't I see it?"

"*Pregúntale a tu Dios*," Claudia said. Ask your God.

I said goodnight and walked toward the glass doors of the hotel. The car slid away, and for a moment I saw myself against the red clay of the prison wall, reaching out. Then I was inside. Marcos gave me the key, and I stumbled through the lobby. The ceiling was dark and bright. As I climbed the stairs, I could feel something breaking loose, and I had scarcely entered the room before I was running for the sink. The avalanche of vomit seemed to have no end. As I gripped the sink, my weight broke the calking and the basin sagged. I sat back against the wall. A heavy mass was growing in my head, like an eggplant dangling from a tiny stem. The stench cut through the delirium, and I stood. The mass swayed behind my eyes. I steadied myself against the wall and began the slow business of cleaning up, leaving a mound of towels below the ruined sink.

For the next three days every task required a Herculean effort. Time slowed. Sitting up in bed took forever. Then the shower, the lesson plans, the walk to school. I pushed my public face through the routine, distant voices echoing. Now two students fighting, like a sudden burst of flame. The leaden mass rocking behind my eyes. My own voice strange in my ears, as if I were speaking through a tube.

I made plans to leave in July at the quarter's end. Meetings were arranged. Lupe tried guilt. "You're leaving us in the ditch!" Then she offered more pay and reduced hours. When that did not persuade me, she said, "Well, it's a shame about Ana. I would not want to be you."

The last two months rose up and fell away. The hills turned gray with winter. I was less anesthetized to trouble, and sometimes the cold reality was harder to take, but there was also comfort in its certainty. I continued to run, now for the pleasure of it. Before I had covered the same distance every day as fast as my body would allow, but now I jogged past the green 6k sign to the 8k, the 9k, and beyond. I indulged in fry bread on rainy days and bought *pascualina* for lunch, a crispy spinach pastry with a boiled egg in the middle. Empanadas and *hambuergesas* found their way back onto my plate. Now and then I even sipped a little whiskey. Road trips to Montevideo with Claudia helped me grow back into a whole life. But I never saw Ana again, and not once did I pray.

It would be wrong to say that lost love and a group of bratty kids took away my faith. That shift had begun years earlier, and it took many months after I returned home for the weight of it to sink in. Yet grief was a mirror, and I could not ignore the man who kept appearing in it. He had been there all along. Now there was no denying this self that could break, no way to make prayers ring true when the body refused to feel more than its flesh. No single cataclysm, just a series of humiliations breaking over my thoughts like water against stone. A steady reduction.

July came, and I left without fanfare. On the last day I rose an hour before dawn, dropped my key on the bed, and struggled through the glass doors with my bags, laboring through the cold to the bus station. Drowsing all the way to Montevideo, my neighbors' heads bobbing in their seats. Then another bus to the airport and a deliciously empty hour to wait for the flight. I was suddenly rich with time. As the plane taxied and rose over the *jacaranda* trees lining the city streets, I looked out across the Rio de la Plata, where the brown water emptied into the South Atlantic, and at last felt something like *tranquilidad*.

Today when I imagine the picnic table in Tennessee and see those two kids sitting beneath the sycamore, the boy leaning in with a whisper and the girl tossing her head back in glee, it is hard to believe they could grow so distant they would no longer speak. But if the choices were weighed against the odds, how could they choose differently? The boy would surely be as much a fool for playing it safe as for boarding the plane out of hope. And the girl, belly growing with a new moon, how could she know what the end of this would be? There it is in the glowing smoke above their table, streaming from the bright eyes of their cigarettes, that vaporous faith. Then they rise, hand in hand, and make their way to her dormitory. One last embrace. Lilac in her hair. *Buenas noches, Juan. Y tú, Ana.* And the parting, each body drawing its own breath.

PART THREE

TEN

Selway by Headlamp

Twelve miles up the potholed road from Lowell, Idaho, the gravel fans into a parking lot where the Selway Trail begins. Horse droppings and cigarette butts litter the ground. A Dodge truck sits near the empty hitching rail where a gray trailer looms against the fir trees, its windows gaping at the oncoming dusk. The river rolls with the sound of a great body moving through grass.

It is midsummer, my second year managing trails in the Selway-Bitterroot Wilderness. I have just parked the government truck near the trailhead where I set off with the crew in June each year, hiking twenty-six miles to the Moose Creek cabin, where we stay until August. In the years since leaving Uruguay, as I've returned to Nebraska for a doctorate, I've resumed my migratory dance between the mountains and plains, trading firefighting for wilderness trails, circling back to my books every fall. I'm glad to be studying Cather again, exploring her letters and manuscripts in the library archive. Teaching Composition to first-years in Lincoln is a snap compared to the sixth-graders I weathered in Minas. After the first week, my students lounge, one at a time, in a tattered chair with broken springs in the office I share with three other TAs, and we listen to Tom Waits as I look over their first drafts and get to know where they're from and what they hope to take from our class.

It's the memory of these heart-to-hearts that has drawn me back to teaching, the long talks I had with my Cather professor, Sue. She discovered Cather while writing her dissertation on *Tristram Shandy*, when stealing time from her research to read *A Lost Lady* and *Lucy Gayheart* brought her a sense of holiday. Reading Cather was something Sue did purely for herself, and I saw how trusting that original pleasure had allowed her to live out what she loved professionally. The trips I took to Red Cloud with classmates as a master's student sparked a kinship I'd never found anywhere else, and I'm grateful to be grounded in that community again. Yet I still yearn for the Northwest every summer, for the crags and rivers that draw me out of myself into the surface of my flesh. Wilderness is a sanctuary where I shed literary theory like a nymphal skin, swinging a pick mattock until my shoulders ache, sitting motionless for an hour at sunset, gazing down on Moose Creek from a high-country camp, where I can trace the drainage basin down to the Selway Canyon and westward, out of sight. I count these watersheds, mountains, and trails among the only true things in my life, and I'm jealous of anything that draws me away.

But next year I'll graduate, and the job prospects look grim, so I've sacrificed a four-day weekend to hike out and catch a flight to Oregon for a conference to read a paper I hope to publish this fall. And now I'm hiking back in to rejoin my crew at the Moose Creek cabin before we set off on our next ten-day hitch.

It's a long way to the cabin from the trailhead, over seven hours in daylight, but I have decided to walk the distance in the dark because I am worried about my sister. She called as I waited for my return flight in Eugene. "He's behind on child support again," she said. "But I don't think I can afford more lawyer's fees." Tonight, as I linger in the breeze rising with the river's chill, I see the shadow of her divorce playing over the surface of the water. Better to get the blood churning in my legs than to toss all night and start, drowsy, at dawn. When I set out along a trail burdened with trouble, I also carry faith that the rise of the slope will creep into my spirits. There is no end to western trails, winding up one mountain and down the next, looping back like infinity. But following a familiar path to my destination can bring an end to worry.

An hour of daylight remains as I shrug into my pack and begin. The first few miles are a wreckage of puddles and ruts where mules have savaged the ground. Hopping along the grassy berm, sometimes leaping across the trough to keep my boots clear of the mud, I consider the night ahead. There are risks. Rattlesnakes thrive along the river, and they often coil in the trail at night. It is too late to raise the dispatcher on the handheld radio. If I fall, no one will think to look for me until tomorrow evening. I accept the risks because I do not believe staying alive is the mark of a good life. Walking in the dark I might see a new thing.

Across the river the needlepoint tops of the tamaracks stand against the fading sky. A campfire glows ahead, the sad eyes of a dog and the shapes of a man and a woman gleaming in its light. I call out to them and they let me go without a word. A tiny gas stove hisses at their feet beneath a steel pot. The buttery smell of their dinner washes over my face as I pass. Beyond the rim of firelight I switch on my headlamp, and the world is reduced to the sweep of its beam.

The silhouettes of the lovers ripple over my thoughts as I go. I see them wherever I look, like spots burned into my eye after a sudden flash. Each present moment seems superimposed by the past.

When I was six or seven years old, my mother left my father. I remember how the house felt without her: the way it feels to watch rain streaming down the windows without turning on the lights, the way some winter days seem to break without dawn. And I recall bumping along the mountain roads in my father's pickup looking for her. My sister sat between us. We watched hills of purple fireweed roll by, saw the churn of Kootenai Falls, spun through the parking lots at all of the trailheads where my father thought she might have gone to think things through. The next day my mother came back and our lives went on as before. Recalling this now, I understand why my sister first resisted all talk of divorce. She imagined her son in the pickup and the empty house. She saw my mother's return.

Night has fallen now. The circle of light dances ahead of my feet. I step into a clearing where knapweed has choked the underbrush. A wooden sign rolls into view. It marks the trail junction at Cupboard Creek, and I know I have twenty more miles to go.

The horizon has nearly lost its dimensions. I can just make out the canyon walls flanking the river channel, the opposing ridgelines rising like a raven's wings. Strange how the view alters in the dark, how familiar things take on new shapes. I have walked this trail dozens of times by daylight, yet I must learn it again. Six more miles to the Pinchot Grade, where I will climb hundreds of feet out of the canyon. I press ahead, hoping memory will serve me well.

———————

My sister met her husband in Mississippi while she was finishing an Art degree and sorting boxes for UPS. He was the sorter, she the loader. They worked well together as he shouted out zip codes while she shuffled packages on the conveyer belt. It must have felt familiar to her, like snapping green beans at the kitchen table, our mother ferrying the heaped bowls to the canner boiling on the stove, like the long mornings we spent as a family cleaning huckleberries by hand after a day on the mountain, our father measuring the purple mounds into gallon-sized freezer bags. Work was our family pastime and our only metaphor for love.

After my parents attended a marriage retreat, my mother posted a card to the refrigerator. Against a red checkered background the script said, "Love is a decision." Love was the decision to return for the holidays, to pull the jars of green beans from the shelf, to hike a mile up the mountain behind the house searching for the right Christmas tree. When my sister brought her husband home after they had eloped, she brought the project of their love. Her job was to say, "Baby, could you wash while I dry?" His job was to play along. Our job was to ignore the muffled shouts behind the bedroom door.

I had heard about my great-grandmother's marriages and my aunt's escape from an alcoholic as a young bride. My parents took in friends from time to time—always men—whose wives had left them. "Whoever divorces his wife," my father would paraphrase from the book of Matthew, "except for adultery, commits adultery. And if a woman divorces her husband and remarries, she commits adultery." I had the language for blaming the victims. But I had no words for the landscape of abuse, no sense of the tangled stories and half-truths, the murky war of a custody dispute.

———————

A half moon has risen above the ridge. I have forgotten where I am. The trail winds in and out of dozens of drainages along the Selway channel. In the dark there is no telling them apart. Beads of water glisten on the weeds beneath the beam of the torch. My boots slosh with each step, blisters imminent. The temperature has begun to drop. I will need my jacket soon. Another switchback, another creek. Now a footbridge, but which one? I have never seen this bridge before, not like this. The mountain curves again toward the river. Now I am climbing. Now the slope is falling away. Branches I cannot see rake over my hands.

The sound of water rushes up from the dark. At last I have reached the log bridge before the Pinchot grade. Somewhere up on the hillside is the halfway point. As I step heel-to-toe across the log, my arms raised at my sides, the lamp beam catches the creek below and I feel as though I am racing upstream, the way a subway car seems to move when the adjacent train pulls away. Steady now. A few steps and terra firma. Tricky business walking over water in the dark. I cast about in the grass for the trail and find it angling back into the woods. Time to climb.

I take a few switchbacks in the river bottom and hit the long sidehill angling out of the canyon. The land pushes against my boots as the slope steepens. I settle into the rhythm of breathing. The smell of pine rises from the mud. A line from Camus drifts to mind: "The struggle itself toward the heights is enough to fill a man's heart."

At the crest, where the grade drops away from my feet, I switch off my headlamp. Stars leap from the sky. A coyote calls far away, and the world opens up again. The heavens shimmer as if a searchlight is rolling over the void. I can see the Seven Persons and Night Red Light, Blackfoot deities presiding over the vision quest. What else is the daily march toward nothingness but a search for good medicine, clear waking dreams, and a story to live by?

Got to keep moving. I flip on the torch and stumble down the descent. Soon the plank bridge at Three Links Creek surfaces in my beam. I finish my last quart, the cool flood spreading throughout my chest, and kneel at the water's edge to refill. An icy draft blows along the creek. I shrug into my jacket and eat a handful of cashews. Thirteen miles down. Fatigue echoes in the small of my back. It is nearly midnight. I decide to push ahead to the Meeker Creek bridge and take my rest there. As I approach the witching hour, I face the worst memories.

By the time my nephew was three years old, my sister had given up her art shows. The easel sat on the concrete floor of her basement near a stack of unfinished oils and watercolors. Her brushes stiffened and dried. The corn in her garden grew tall instead.

That summer was the beginning of the end. I came to visit in August after a year away, eager to pull weeds among the peppers, enact the family ritual. One night, as we all sat drinking coffee on the back porch and listening to the crickets, I thought of visiting Yaak Falls.

"If the sun is out we can go for a swim," I said. "The water should be low enough by now."

"Not with my son." My brother-in-law sat with his back to me.

"We'll be careful," I said. "There's a natural pool downstream that kids play in all the time."

"No. Not with my boy."

"What do you mean 'your boy'? He's my nephew, for God's sake. You can't keep him cooped up in the backyard all summer."

"No. Period. And that goes for her, too." He stood and walked into the house. She followed him without a word.

———————

I am counting the landmarks. Four miles to Tango Creek, then one more to the Meeker bridge. Little things loom large. One of my heels is heating up. A sure blister as soon as I stop. The wet pants chafe my thighs. *Snake!* I leap back. False alarm—a brown stem twisted in the path. Jumpy now. Jittery. *Too far to go yet for that. Think. Snakes hate mud.* But what else lurks out there in the cackling dark?

Old fears mingle with the new. I glimpse the moon gliding through the pines like Lorca's moon in *Blood Wedding*, when the bride gallops into the forest with her lover, the groom in hot pursuit. The moon cries, "This night there will be sweet blood for my cheeks." Death appears as a beggar woman in the woods, and she calls on the moon to keep the lovers from escaping their fate. She sings: "The river's whisper will muffle the torn flight of their shrieks." I dream I am running through Lorca's woods. The pine grove echoes with crashes and shouts. My boots drum ahead like hooves. I am the bride and the lover and the groom.

I wrote to her as soon as I returned home: "How long has he had you shut up in the house? You've got to stand up for yourself."

He wrote back: "Protecting my wife is my business, not yours. No one lives with her but me and our son. I don't want you putting ideas in her head."

He was reading her messages. Things were worse than I'd thought.

My reply: "'Protecting' your wife becomes my business when your wife is my sister and your control interferes with her life. I will defend her right to privacy and freedom. You have no right to deny her that."

Still nothing from her, so I called.

"What's going on? Can you talk, or is he home?"

"It's OK," she said, "but I wish you wouldn't write. It makes everything worse."

"Makes what worse?"

"He hasn't hit me yet, but he's thrown me by my hair twice."

"What? That bastard. I had no idea."

"I'm scared. The other day I was walking out of the bathroom and he bumped me with his hip and I fell down. He said, 'Look—I can knock you over with nothing but my skinny little ass.' And he wakes me at three in the morning by licking me. Sometimes he's on top of me before I'm even awake. He's done that before, but now it happens every day. It's freaking me out."

My headlamp jags among the cedars. The moon races alongside. The woods echo with the peals of my footsteps, the trail corridor yawning like an open tomb.

A white body leaps toward my face. I fall back shouting. With one arm shielding my eyes, I train the beam on the ghostly orb of a spider's web. It glistens there as I catch my breath. The damp ground seeps through my jeans, and I surface from my dream.

She refused to leave. He was trying to do better, she said. Things would work out. Love was a decision.

I read everything I could find about domestic violence: the wheel of power, the isolation, the intimidation, the guilt, the victim's denial. I murdered him hundreds of times in my sleep. "It's not about you," my friend Martha told me. "It's about your sister gaining control of her life. You've got to break the isolation wall first. Whatever you lose in pride, she gains in support."

So I called all of the family friends, told them about the hair pulling and the licking and the prison of that house. They wrung their hands and said they were sorry. And went about their lives. "God hates divorce," one woman told my grandmother in the grocery store. My grandmother had also been unsympathetic to my aunt when her drunk husband was beating her two weeks into their marriage. "You wanted this," she had told my aunt. "Live with it." But there in the produce aisle, listening to that tired line and remembering her daughter running from her cabin through fresh snow after calling for help, my grandmother finally raised her voice and said, "I'm sure God does. But that's not all he hates."

After many tense weeks, a few friends helped my sister orchestrate a legal separation. It was October. Tires crunched over the leaves as they arrived, followed at last by the highway patrol. Flanked by two paunchy officers, she served him the papers and the restraining order, then— because she had no legal right to her son and no proof of the danger he faced—she walked alone down the driveway and slid into the back seat of the deputy's car.

———

I hear Tango Creek babbling ahead. One more mile to Meeker. My heel throbs with each step. The tip of my nose has gone numb and both knees have begun to stiffen. In the pale glow of my watch, I see it is nearly 2:00. As the trail winds in and out of the drainages along the river, I try to summon the bridge. *Meeker. Meeker.* And there it is rising out of the darkness, thumping underfoot. I switch off the headlamp, sink to my knees, and roll onto my back. Blood surges into my feet.

A thick canopy of cedar and fir arches overhead. Almost pitch black. The moon is nowhere to be seen. Nothing but the roar of the water below.

I nurse my blister and raw inner thighs, cinch down the hood of my jacket. The planks are hard and cold against my back. Eighteen miles down. Another eight or so left. I let out a sigh, and then sleep sweeps over me.

———————

An hour later I wake, shivering. Must be forty degrees. Standing is difficult. The blister stings, and little stabs of pain shoot through my knees. I touch my toes a few times, do a couple of slow lunges, and get down to business.

I begin to think that this nighttime hike is my attempt to understand divorce—what it is to meet old friends and find no warmth in their faces, to walk among familiar landmarks as a stranger. And this brutal stretch, when I know the worst is behind but must walk in pain because I would otherwise die of the cold—this must be at least a shadow of the reality check after the papers are served, when the wave of pent up anguish breaks.

This is what my sister has been trying to explain, this self-contained hell. Living with relatives. Looking for work. Trying the patience of the few friends left: a little babysitting here, a dinner there, until the doors close. In place of fear, just a life grinding itself into dust. The indifferent world. Lie down in it too long and say goodbye.

I know I have reached Cedar Flats when I see a bare patch on the forest floor where nothing but clover and trilliums grow. I recall lying here with heat cramps during my first hike up the Selway. A flicker of dread passes through me. There's something unearthly about the place in the half-light of the headlamp. But it's too late for fear. If the moon wants my blood, she can have it—alms for the beggar woman called Death. I push ahead.

Damn these drainages. Always curving back into the mountain, then out toward the river, like the folds of a giant dress. I'm stumbling now, catching a rock and lunging blindly ahead while my thoughts turn to static. My toes are cold, but my heels are burning.

Something is happening along the ridgetop. A tiny hint of blue and green up there among the shadows. Daybreak. And around the bend, another drainage: Divide Creek.

I don't bother walking over the flimsy bridge. My feet are already as wet as they can be. Swish, splash, and I'm across. Maybe a mile and a half left. Still too dark to walk without my torch, but there's sky overhead again. I'm limping like a geezer to the chow line. Pancake breakfast waiting there. Butter and syrup. And an egg, if I can scavenge one from the propane fridge.

Miles away, my sister stirs in her sleep. A flicker of worry crosses her face, a crease deepening between her eyebrows. Things are not as simple as a hike through the woods. Dawn is not so soft when it pulls the curtain away from misery. My nephew is gone on visitation this weekend, and she will wake alone, brew some coffee, pick up a few stray toys. Cradling a steaming cup, she will notice mold along the wall and think of the cough she has not been able to shake for weeks. Three bulging garbage bags wait near the door for the laundromat. As she stands from the table, stepping out onto the frigid stoop of her apartment, she will wonder why taking control of her life has left her feeling so powerless. *Be free,* they say: *chase your dream.* She will take a few breaths of mold-free air and brace herself for the day.

Before long the timbers of the Moose Creek bridge loom over me and I'm turning the corner, taking a sidelong glance toward the junction with the Selway—just light enough now to see the color of the water against the solid backdrop of fir trees—then duck-walking up the switchbacks that lead to a grass airstrip a hundred feet out of the canyon. Fatigue has cleansed the earth. I will think soon enough of my hand in my sister's divorce. Then my nephew will stand before me as myself waking to find my mother gone. The moon will return to haunt my steps. But now I am nearing the end of this hike, closing in on the sweet illusion of stepping off a wilderness trail and pretending to have arrived.

Soon I roll over the rim of the canyon onto the airstrip. White-tailed deer bob along the edge of the runway. Elk glide through the trees like ghosts. A quarter mile of knee-high grass stretches out before me. I switch off my headlamp. In the early light I can see the mules grazing at the edge of the corral. Bailey Mountain towers in the distance. The world brightens with each step I take. Three hundred yards. A hundred. Then the log walls of the cabin unfold among the trees, and I walk through the old wooden gate into the dawn.

The Tao of River Trash

Ev'n from the tomb the voice of nature cries,
Ev'n in our ashes live their wonted fires.

THOMAS GRAY

Awesterner steeped in timbered ridgelines and thousands of acres of
wilderness might, at first glance, regard Iowa as a lost landscape,
all ploughed under and fouled, like Leopold's nightmare of a place and
time when the young would have no country to be young in. That pretty
much summed up my view when I first arrived in Pella, Iowa, for a visiting position at Central College. I enjoyed a good rapport with colleagues
and students, but after returning to the mountains every summer for
nearly a decade to work with the Forest Service, I hoped to settle somewhere west of the plains. Since I didn't plan on staying in Pella for more
than a year or two, I signed a lease on an apartment in Prairie Village,
a former retirement community that could not keep pace with its turn-
over rate and had begun recruiting younger tenants. The complex was a
warren of ranch-style rentals with a central laundry facility and mailroom,
which both smelled of urine. I often fled to the bike path—out of town to
the Des Moines River—and in some of the wooded stretches of the trail I
could almost forget where I was. In truth, it was difficult to take in what I
saw. Corn stood along the highways like prison bars, and the river bore the
filth of the feedlots upstream.

In time I would find wildness in Iowa: the sky darkening beneath
a funnel cloud at midday, oaks and maples whipping in violent wind. I
would remember what I knew from Cather's fiction, that the uplift I had
felt on granite peaks might be a frame of mind capable of illuminating any
place. But because I had been raised in the solitude of cedars and pines, my
first stance toward the prairie was retreat.

After I recognized the flights out and back on the bike as little more than exercise in a giant cage, it seemed wise to seek a new center, and so I became a harvester of river trash. The idea struck when I happened by a coworker's office and saw a photo on her wall of a glass bottle nearly buried in dirt and gravel, a thick colony of clover growing from the soil inside. Beads of moisture hung from the glass above the clover. The slant of light appeared to be mid-morning. Transfixed by the little field of green straining skyward with nowhere to go, I imagined the sun passing its zenith, heat building beneath the glass until the clover wilted and collapsed. When I asked who had snapped the photo, she said, "Oh, that's my husband, Ken's. He likes to walk along the river watching for things that wash up on the bank. He has a whole series of those." He did, indeed—an orange bobber glowing beneath receding ice, a doll's head topsy-turvy in tall grass, a shoe buried sole-up in oak leaves. My impulse was to look away from litter at the river's edge, offended by the eyesore, but here was a different way of seeing. I began to wonder what I was missing right under my nose.

Ken said if I liked his photos I ought to look up his friend David, who runs a river cleanup each year and builds a sculpture at the Iowa State Fair with scrap metal salvaged from the water. David looks like a Harley rider with his barrel chest and beefy arms. "I love coming home after a long road trip," he says. "Driving down out of South Dakota into the cornfields, that rolling, sexy loam . . . mmmhhh." David's art studio, which was once his home, is built entirely of refuse, a hardwood floor recycled from an old gymnasium, and most of the lumber scavenged from driftwood or collapsed barns. Each of his sculptures tells the story of water conservation in the form of a giant water droplet made of rebar and steel, or great rusted oars fashioned from an abandoned car frame, or an iron bicycle seat and gears welded into the shape of a fish. Searching for footing on the prairie, I am fortunate to have found these two guides—Ken with his camera and David with his forge and acetylene torch—who can stare down a car frame rusting in a river and see more than a lost cause. Even here, they suggest, a raw beauty might be found, and this is not to ignore the ruin so much as to bear witness to it with love and sorrow.

So it is with fear and hope that I set off on a sunny day in April, with a blue vault of sky overhead and a southern wind gusting off the water, to harvest trash with my first group of student volunteers. Every spring

Central College sponsors a service day on which classes are canceled and all members of the campus community are encouraged to join one of the twenty or so projects organized by nonprofits in Pella and a few surrounding towns. I have volunteered to lead a project upriver of the Red Rock Dam, where the U.S. Army Corps of Engineers has marked a stretch of shoreline to be cleaned. Lake Red Rock, named for the town it flooded when the dam was built in 1969, is the largest lake in Iowa, running about eleven miles northwest along the Des Moines River watershed. Despite the gnawed look of the clay banks, where the water level can fluctuate by more than thirty feet throughout the year, the shoreline at Red Rock can be a fine place to walk, as I and my group of students discover while scouring the water's edge. As much as the tires, bottles, and propane tanks littering the shore confirm my worst suspicions of Iowa waterways, the energy of the group wakes a different yearning, and I begin to understand that this attempt to leave the lake better than we found it might mean more than climbing a backcountry peak for the view. As we comb the shoreline, I feel our common cause rising in my chest like a buoy.

There are a few rules for harvesting trash, as I have explained to my team of volunteers: Plastics such as drinking bottles and milk jugs should be drained and separated for recycling, so long as they are not filled with sludge or slime. Anything like a propane tank or an aerosol can with a hose attached, a bluish valve, or milky residue should be left untouched and reported to the local police as possible methamphetamine gear. If the recyclables and trash can be bagged in different colors, so much the better.

Each castaway item has a story: a flip-flop with a pregnancy kit, a yellow Pennzoil bottle, a foam smiley face from a boat antenna. Tires and propane tanks pile up by the dozens. Sometimes a refrigerator finds its way downstream. Where does it all come from? What is the story? After years of practicing the wilderness ethic of invisibility, I struggle to decipher this new text scribbled over the shoreline. It is too easy to dismiss it as the general flotsam and jetsam of the marketplace. What I need is expansion, a larger view. "The eye is the first circle," Emerson writes; "the horizon which it forms is the second." As I walk the shoreline, searching (almost hoping) for trash, I begin to think of all of the individual choices made, why someone might choose Arrowhead water over Fiji, and why, after buying clean water—after making that conscious choice—one would toss the bottle into the lake. Soda bottles tell a clearer tale, but nearly half the recyclable detritus in Iowa waterways once held commercial drinking water. How can this be?

I picture a man on a boat eating potato salad while watching a heron sail overhead. He drains the last of his Aquafina, and what next? He could toss the bottle in the bottom of the boat or bag it for recycling later, but instead he pitches it into the lake. What I want to know is whether there is any hesitation, whether this is an offhand gesture or whether he studies the water lapping against his boat and contemplates the difference between it and the drinkable sort, whether he is careless or so mindful of place that he deems it lost and incapable of further injury. *An empty bottle won't hurt*, he might think. *This lake is filthy anyway.* Maybe then he tosses the bottle, lies back so the walls of the boat shield him from all but the sky, and rocks to sleep beneath the innocent blue. The man who throws his tires into the river may be past hope (if anyone is truly beyond hope), but it's the man with the bottled water whom I want to understand, because the hieroglyphics of his thoughts might explain this lake, where the pelicans take turns fishing and the mallards flip head down kicking their feet with what could be anguish or glee.

Trash gathering is good for such musings, because it requires little conscious thought. While the students chatter, shaking lake water from Gatorade bottles onto each other, I smile and urge them on and puzzle over the man with the Aquafina. Perhaps he does not know that water quality is more carefully regulated for tap water than for the bottled-water industry, that vast oil resources are needed to manufacture the twenty or thirty billion plastic bottles purchased each year. Would he still make his choice if he knew that producing each bottle of water consumes three to seven times as much water as the bottle contains, or that the exotic places featured on some labels offer potable water to only half their residents, or that he pays one thousand times more for water in a bottle than for a liter from his tap?

What I am trying to learn from river trash is how to see the place this man has shaped. "The heart can be filled anywhere on earth," writes Bill Holm, and I want to harbor that hope. Here on this clay bank where I and my students are now wrestling a buried cable free, here in this pile of driftwood where the water bottles outnumber the empty liters of Mountain

Dew, what can I learn other than despair? What is the story? I hear someone call my name and turn to find a student with his arms full of plastic. As I open my bag, he smiles and drops his burden, and for a moment there is music as his trash drums upon my own. His face reminds me of another young man, and I have a feeling then like the threshold of a dream, when strange images leap together. The open bag gapes like a portal, pulling me in, pitching me back to the summer when I said goodbye to the western woods.

At the start of my last season leading a wilderness crew on the Moose Creek District in Idaho—the summer before I moved to Iowa—I drew the worst team I had ever seen. This was my tenth summer with the Forest Service after six years with the fire crew in Montana, a stint tending mountain bike trails in Colorado, and two seasons as the foreman of wilderness trails on the Selway. Each year I discovered that those assigned to the wilderness crew had no notion of what they were in for and little desire to spend the next three months lugging an eighty-pound pack through the forest while manning one end of a crosscut saw. But recruiting summer staff to clear remote trails was a lower priority for the Forest Service than handling revenue sources like timber contracts. And since budget cuts had whittled the crew to three positions, including mine, it was easiest for my supervisor at Moose Creek to hire from a small pool of returning hands or local college students, hoping I could get them up to speed. So it was that when I arrived for orientation at the start of my final season, I learned I'd be spending the summer with Nat and Brad.

Nat was fresh out of high school, a skinny kid with curly brown hair and a thin beard covering most of his neck. He rolled his own Drum cigarettes, which would have made him seem tough if he could have kept a lid on his nervous laugh. Nat giggled when he had no idea what I was talking about or when he felt anxious or when he wished he could go lie down, which meant he laughed nearly all the time. His father was a professor at Boise State University and kept a cabin near Bonners Ferry, where the two often went to fish. Beyond that he had no backwoods experience.

Brad was a beach bum from California and a two-year veteran at Moose Creek. He'd been assigned to my crew as a demotion from the construction crew, which spent the summer building bridges or retainer walls. His former supervisor tired of Brad's mood swings and passed him on to me with the caveat that he was a good worker but prone to "wigging out" from time to time. Like Nat, Brad seemed an amiable sort at first. He had shoulder-length blond hair, a winsome smile, and the build of a linebacker. But if he had difficulty coping with the construction crew, I thought, the mental strain of three months in the backcountry might prove too great. Trail work was the most physically demanding of the forestry jobs I'd known, and the wilderness crew upped the ante by living in a remote cabin from June to August. It was a steep learning curve for a newbie like Nat, and I feared it would be a recipe for more than one of Brad's meltdowns.

I knew trouble was brewing when we all lined up with the firefighters to take the pack test, a three-mile speed walk on flat ground with a forty-five-pound pack. Those who could not finish in forty-five minutes or less were deemed unfit for fire duty, which was considerably lighter than trail maintenance. A firefighter might dig feverishly for an hour or two to contain a lightning strike, but most days at the fire cache passed as slowly as a tractor through town, whereas trail hands swung an axe or a pick mattock all day. It was a point of pride for us to dust the fire dogs in the pack test. But when Nat and Brad lurched in just under forty-five minutes and spent a few moments yakking in the ditch, their faces lathered in sweat, our prospects as a crew dimmed considerably.

The fact that it rained steadily throughout our first hitch did not improve morale. Water soaked under our tents through the forest duff, leaving our sleeping bags moldy and damp. When we weren't clipping brush from the trail, drenching ourselves each time a waterlogged branch toppled onto our backs, we huddled around our gas stove to warm a batch of noodles or took shelter in our soggy tents. This was a rough introduction to wilderness work, I assured Nat, who looked more haggard each morning. He'd left his cigarettes behind, an error he had discovered after hiking five miles to our first campsite—"Oh, no!" he moaned. "No fucking way! No fucking way!"—and he now had the look of a starving dog, the hollows in his cheeks growing by the day, his eyes bulging like a levee. Gone was his laughter, his boyish grin. Nat now spent the day working a muscle in his jaw while clipping brush, wiping water from his eyes with the back of his wrist. During our breaks he searched the forest floor for hollow twigs, stuffing them with dead grass and huffing what smoke he could from the joint. "This would be a great time to quit," I offered, but Nat seemed to take my meaning wrong, because he packed his things as soon as we returned to the wilderness cabin, lit out for the trailhead, and never looked back.

That left me with Brad for the rest of the summer. The weather improved, as it always did in late June and July. We camped near Grizzly Saddle, where alpenglow throbs in the fir at dusk, where small patches of snow linger in the shade until midsummer. We cleaned waterbars along Moose Ridge, taking turns busting the clods with a pick mattock, then scraping each basin smooth with a shovel so rain could sweep from the trail in a storm. We lingered over dinner at Ditch Creek, the pines creaking overhead while Brad worked himself into rants about the cost of college and how unfair it was that our senators weren't sending their sons or daughters to war and how it was bullshit that a CEO could make three hundred times the average worker's salary and then lay off a thousand people without a second thought. Mostly I agreed with him, nodding as I sipped my tea. These were pleasant moments, the sort I recall now in an attempt at fairness. But more often trouble cast its pall over us.

One day we were walking back to a camp along Bear Creek at the end of our Moose Ridge hitch, a route looping over Grizzly Saddle, down through Ditch Creek, and back up the Selway Trail. Windfalls had been scarce in the creek bottom, where I usually anticipated laboring over a few big cedar with the crosscut and axe, so we had finished a day ahead of schedule. The campsite along Bear Creek was a dream, moss and grass to cushion our tents, easy access to water, ample shade: so enticing that Brad agreed to spend a day exploring a new trail before breaking camp. The next morning we packed only the axe and saw and wandered up the Pettibone Trail, logging out a few fallen trees, taking our time. Brad napped for an hour after lunch as I scouted the huckleberry crop, grubbing morels from punky logs and eating a few service berries.

All was well until we returned to the main trail and began hacking our way through a thick patch of knapweed which had colonized the trail a mile or two from our camp. Knapweed is an invasive species thought to be native to the steppes of Russia. Mule traffic had seeded the entire river trail with it, and this patch was worse than any I'd seen, the vines standing head high and so thick the tread was scarcely visible underfoot. Knapweed has a way of wrapping itself around a hiker's ankles that can be aggravating at the end of the day. The only thing to do is swim through it and hope no rattlesnakes have coiled in the path. This is a challenge while carrying a saw on one shoulder, but I managed as best I could with one free arm.

Brad was having a tough time of it, stumbling and cursing. He fell behind, stopping to vent his rage by swinging the axe blindly about. "Fucking shit!" he yelled. "Son of a bitch!" I forged ahead and his cries began to fade, but then I heard the tattoo of his boots on the trail and realized he was running toward me, thrashing and flailing with the axe. I lunged up the bank to make way and watched him blaze past. The knapweed rippled as he ran, tripping him headlong before he roared back to his feet and charged on, brandishing the axe. I watched him struggle up a small hill, and then he was gone.

Brad's former supervisor had warned me that he might wig out now and then, but I was unprepared for an outburst like this, which sent alarms clanging through my chest. Before continuing I unsheathed the saw in case Brad was lying in wait for me, a scenario which seemed only slightly more bizarre than what I had just witnessed. Gripping the wooden handle with one hand, I laced my other fingers through the grooves in the blade as I advanced, gooseflesh rising along my neck.

When I crested the rise overlooking our camp, Brad was sitting on a log with his back to me, boiling noodles. I stopped, sheathed the saw, and ambled in.

"How's it going?" I asked.

Brad grinned. "Better now. Sorry about that—I just had a mental block or something."

"Jesus, I guess. You can't be swinging the axe around like that."

He straightened on the log and began waving his hands. "I know. It's just that we have to *walk* everywhere, man. Damn, sometimes I just want to hop on my motorcycle and go buy some Ho Hos at the Quickie Mart. You know?"

"Well, yeah," I said, "but what did you expect when you signed up for wilderness trails?"

"I don't know," he said. "I mean, sometimes it feels like I'm trapped out here, like there's no escape. There's *no escape*, man."

"You dumb fucker," I said, "this *is* the escape."

He shook his head. "Sorry, man. I wish I could be your little buddy and all, but I'm just doing this for the cash." I understood that for Brad a Forest Service job meant better pay than anything else he could find for the summer, and I also knew that like me he hadn't been given a choice once his supervisor had passed him on to my crew. But I resented his unwillingness to make the best of it. The rainy season had passed, and we had the heart of summer to look forward to in a million-acre wilderness, tucked miles away from asphalt and roadkill and the incessant buzz of traffic. This was my last season on the Selway before the demands of teaching, attending conferences, and publishing scholarship would consume my summer months. I wanted to savor what little time I had left in the wild.

After Brad finished his dinner and retired to his tent, I boiled a pot of couscous and stirred in a mess of canned salmon, trying to let my anger go. The creek sang at my back. Wind murmured over the grass at the edge of our campsite, where a good-sized meadow stretched out to the trail, the seed heads of the grass like a skim of golden cream. I was looking in that direction, over the log where Brad had been sitting, when a brown wedge-shaped head rose from the grass scarcely ten feet away and began testing the air with its tongue. There is a stab of adrenaline that comes just before the brain can identify a sight or sound, like the split second of alarm between a snap in the house at night and the thought of roof timbers settling. And then, sometimes, a flood of dread follows, when the brain knows it should be afraid. I normally let snakes slither from the trail when we came upon them, but I had never seen one in camp before. It was a timber rattler as thick as my wrist, a barklike calico covering its skin. I thought of letting it go, but the more I considered the grassy flat between our camp and the trail, the less I wanted to watch for it underfoot the next morning.

Armed with a shovel and still upset with Brad, I began stalking the snake. It backed into a grove of seedling pines, coiling and lifting its head, tongue flickering. I dropped the head of the shovel inches away, as a test. It drew back, hissing and rattling, two curved fangs glistening in its pink mouth. It was not until I poked it with the blade that the snake struck, its head pinging against the steel before it broke for better cover. I ran along behind, amazed by its length—five or six feet—but now more determined than ever to finish the deed. When it coiled against a log, I braced myself, gripped the shovel handle at its tip, and pinned the snake to the ground, grinding the blade through its flesh as the rattler struck the handle again and again, finally sinking its teeth into the wood in exhaustion. Blood welled up along the spade, the tail writhing long after the eyes had dimmed. Prying the head from the shovel handle with a stick, I chopped at the neck to be sure, stepping shakily away from the scene to watch the body worming into itself while the head sat alone, half buried, the jaws working like the beak of a thirsty bird. As I stood there, legs gone to jelly, my anger gave way to sadness. Rattlesnakes were part of the wild, part of the sinuous body of the forest I claimed to love, and whatever reasons I might muster for killing a snake in camp, I knew I had lashed out from frustration at Brad's refusal to see this place—my refuge—as anything but a prison.

We broke camp the next morning, shouldered our packs, and hiked back to the cabin for our days off. Brad seemed shaken by his breakdown in the knapweed, as if he had reached a mental threshold then and crossed over. He locked himself in a bunkhouse for hours, appearing only to smoke on the withered stoop or to boil a pot of chili on the propane stove. I coaxed him out to play cards a few times and took him to a swimming hole one afternoon, but he seemed determined to brood, counting the days to the summer's end. Over the next few weeks I watched Brad shut himself behind the barricade of his own thoughts, as I had done in Uruguay.

We muddled ahead, finally setting off on our last hitch along the Big Rock Trail, which would lead us to the wilderness boundary. Tension had been simmering between us all along as Brad continued to chafe against the heat and mosquitoes and his ongoing sense of entrapment. But with the end of the season within reach, I endured his complaints without comment, thinking the worst was past. Our fireside chats over the summer confirmed that Brad's father had schizophrenia, and I learned that his mother had also grown delusional over the years, speaking to an imaginary friend in the backyard while watering her flowers. This kept me watchful. More than once, cocooned in my sleeping bag at night, I woke with alarm when he unzipped his tent and stepped outside. So my belly washed cold one morning when Brad began weeping into his oatmeal bowl, cursing our boss for sending peaches and cream instead of the apple-cinnamon flavor he'd ordered. I said nothing, but I sensed a storm about to break.

Later that day we were clipping brush in ninety-degree heat, swatting at horseflies, when Brad suddenly threw down his loppers and said, "Fuck this, I quit."

I straightened and wiped my forehead, grimacing as the sweat stung my eyes. "What's that?"

"I quit. Fuck you and fuck this job." We were working near the top of the ridge, looking down on the Selway watershed and out over many mountain ranges to the south and west, toward the Salmon and the Payette. It took me a moment to realize what Brad had said as his red face came into focus, a strand of hair clinging to his sweaty cheek.

"OK," I said slowly, "but where are you going to go? We're fifteen miles in, and it's only thirteen miles to the end of the trail. If you went back to the cabin, you'd have to walk an extra twenty-six miles out along the river. We've only got five days left, for Christ's sake."

He considered this. "Well, I don't know, but I'm sure as shit not going to clip any more of this fucking brush. Why do you care about all this? Who's going to know the difference? We should be swimming every day, soaking up some rays, not slaving away on this bullshit."

I could feel my face heating up. "I care because whoever rides a horse this way, even if it's just one of the rangers or an outfitter, will know a trail crew was out here this summer, and some of them will know it was us. Besides, it's our job—we're not getting paid to jack off."

"You're so full of shit," he said. "You just want to make me suffer."

"Give me a break, man. You've been railing all summer about these greedy executives who take everybody's money and then cut and run before the shit hits the fan. How are you any different? You want to fuck around and get paid for it—leave the mess on the trail and hightail it before you get caught."

His face crumpled, and he sobbed, "But I just need the money. I'm way in debt for college. This is the only thing I can do other than washing dishes. Why are you such a bastard?"

I shrugged and waved my pruners at the brush. "I know this isn't fun, but it's got to be done, and that's what we promised to do when we signed up this summer. Look, if you want to quit, go ahead. But I'm not packing your crap out of here. Take the day off. Go back to camp and sleep on it if you want—I'll leave you on the clock. We can talk about it tonight."

He nodded at that, tears streaking his cheeks, and disappeared around the bend. I had a satellite phone in my pack, which was to be reserved for emergencies, and I decided to use it. After this latest collapse, I wasn't sure if Brad had much pride left. What calculus might spin in his thoughts if he believed he had nothing to lose? So I called our supervisor, got him to promise to leave a truck at the trailhead the next day in case we needed to hike out early, and said I'd keep him apprised if things took a turn for the worse.

When I returned to camp that evening, Brad sat hunched on a stump, his bleached hair covering his face. I told him we could leave the next day if he really couldn't stick it out. I'd been there myself a time or two, I said, and I'd understand if he'd reached his limit. He brightened at that, wiping his swollen eyes.

We shouldered our packs the next morning in a thick fog. By midday the sun was bright overhead, but a thunder cell built behind the ridge as we switchbacked down to a creek bottom. The smell of ozone hung in the air. We were only six miles from the trailhead, but the clouds looked swollen and dark. It seemed best to make camp and ride out the storm. Almost as soon as we had pitched our tents, the sky darkened and the wind blew hard out of the north. A chill fell over the drainage, hail pelting us as we dove into our tents, lying ten yards apart while the storm howled and thunder cracked overhead. I fell asleep to the drumming hail and woke to birdsong, the dome of my tent glowing in the afternoon light.

Brad gave some thought to his plight during the storm, because he offered over dinner that we wouldn't have to leave the next morning. He might have apologized, or perhaps I want to remember it this way, but the essential fact is that we stayed to the bitter end. When we hiked out to the truck on the last day, climbing a few hundred feet out of the creek bottom, I took huge strides up the slope, my chest burning as Brad fell behind. Once we'd turned in our gear, we never spoke again. I moved to Iowa and ended my Forest Service career, thinking of mountains as I drove through the cornfields in August, the road like a corridor between jail cells, Brad's voice echoing in my thoughts. *There's no escape, man. No escape.* I unloaded my things at the rental in Prairie Village, stepped over to the mailroom with its faint odor of colostomy bags, and returned to my ranch-style cave, where I drew the shades, packed a lip full of Copenhagen, and tried to forget where I was.

Now I am standing on the shore of Lake Red Rock looking into the eyes of a young man who has been searching for water bottles all afternoon as if for treasure. I hear shouts all along the shore. "Look what I found." "Can you believe it? Who would throw a propane tank in the river?" "Oh, wait, let's check the nozzle. Nope, not blue, must be safe." "Crazy!" When we gather the group at the end of the day for a picnic lunch, I still have to pick a few Gatorade bottles off the grass before we load the vans, and I know that while many will grumble about missing Sunday football, others will never look at a water bottle the same way again. I think once more of Emerson: "Our life is an apprenticeship to the truth that around every circle another can be drawn; that there is no end in nature, but every end is a beginning; that there is always another dawn risen on mid-noon, and under every deep a lower deep opens." Then I remember my answer to Brad after his struggle through the knapweed, how impatient I was with his inability to see that wilderness might offer more than exile, yet how easily I slipped into the same way of thinking about Iowa.

After surrendering the faith I had struggled to hold as a child, I thought wilderness might be all there was to live for, the immutable stone of self upon which all the other shadows danced, the great escape. But a lot depends on how large a circle I want to draw around what I see. Widening the horizon I fashion for myself begins with the question: could *this* be the escape? And then it is no longer about flight. The smaller circles nest within the new.

Driving away from Lake Red Rock in a van packed with volunteers, I sense that buoy rising in my chest once more. Right here, I wonder—with the happy rumble of talk, the snapping bubble gum, the strange fusion of sweat and shampoo—could this be a way for the heart to be filled? There are enough outcasts howling in the western woods, enough dirges being sung, enough prophecies snapping in the wind. I look into the eyes of young people who have only reservoirs to be young in, and while

I hope for something better for them, I see also the resiliency of youth, how the human spirit can seek its own level like water, adopting the shape of its place. In the cornfields, which still hold the tallgrass prairie in topsoil built over millennia of broken-down bluestem and coneflowers, I see a touchstone for myself. Through friends like Ken and David I feel my circles expand. In the fall and spring I cycle out to the Red Rock Dam and watch the pelicans take turns fishing, forty or fifty birds standing for hours in a tight pack on a sandbar while a dozen others flap out to the tailwaters to feast on stunned carp. Most of the flock leaves in June and returns in September, but a few stay year round, suffering right through the heat and the ice and the subzero winds. *Even in our ashes*, I think. If the pelicans can love this river, so can I.

TWELVE

Down from the Mountaintop

I t was March, the beginning of autumn in Uruguay, where I had been teaching for a few months, and I was chatting on a stone patio with Sam and Susan, a couple from Seattle. We sat looking out on a sheep ranch, pasture rippling away on all sides, a grassy saddle rising in the distance. Mariela, a colleague at St. Catherine's School, invited me to this nineteenth-century *estancia* whenever she and her husband hosted tourists from England or the United States. This meant an evening in the countryside, a meal of carne asada, and conversations on the patio, where I earned my supper by putting travelers at ease.

Susan had been regaling us with tales of hiking the Cascade Mountains, and I mentioned missing the wilderness peaks in Montana, where I could look down on the ridgelines and valleys shaped by mountain streams, see how they fit together, and feel the world stretching out simplified and whole. My earliest memories were forged on a mountain, my childhood home overlooking the Kootenai River Valley a thousand feet above the town of Troy. From the breakfast table each morning I could see rusty train cars winding along the river far below, the engine whistle rising like a songbird's trill. No matter where I went in those days, the road always led back up, back home. So my urge to climb was as much a desire to reenact that ritual of return as it was a search for transcendence. Susan's talk of the Cascades reminded me how keen my yearning for home had become in a flat and foreign land.

Sam gazed at the pasture as we talked. He'd grown up hiking in Oregon, but had worked in Seattle for almost twenty years as a computer programmer. He smiled as we chattered on, and then he said, "After a while you stop looking for that mountaintop."

I wasn't sure if Sam intended this as a lament, but it struck me as a terrifying thought. What would life be without the mountaintop? I stared at the sheep, heads bent to the ground, ambling blindly through the grass, and wondered if it might be a little like that.

I knew that the fever for conquest drawing other climbers up a sheer mountain face, sacrificing fingers and toes to the bitter wind, was different from my own urge to buck gravity. Ropes, crampons, and ice axes held no appeal—I hiked toward the summit to rediscover the vantage from which I knew myself, to recapture the sense of belonging I'd felt as a child after riding the school bus up from the valley and bursting through my front door. Shortly after I arrived in Uruguay, my parents sent word they were renting out the old place in Montana and moving away, so Sam's words pricked the nagging fear that my point of origin could be lost, that it was already slipping away.

As I threw myself into my lessons, rising early each day to prepare and sinking to sleep late every night, the memory of my conversation with Sam cast a pall over the gentle hills and plains surrounding me. By the time I said farewell to Uruguay at the end of the term in July, I was dreaming of snowcapped peaks like I might thirst for cold lemonade on a summer day. Following a friend's lead, I set off for a Forest Service job near Winter Park, intent on wearing my boot soles smooth traversing the Rocky Mountain high country.

Moving to Colorado, home to more than fifty peaks above 14,000 feet, only intensified my trust in the mountaintop. Even driving west out of Denver and climbing through Genesee toward Evergreen brought that feeling of uplift. And when I settled in the town of Fraser for my summer job, I lived for burning lungs and wobbling knees, grinding up steep trails on my mountain bike and pounding out miles along the Continental Divide.

The paradox I kept dodging on the mountaintop was that I thought it should be mine, alone, or at least mine when no one else was around. The stream of recreation traffic from Denver each weekend should have reminded me that I was among kindred spirits, but instead it reinforced my need for solitude. I'd seen a similar tendency in ski shops, staff babbling in some secret code of the trade to remind themselves they were different from the schmucks picking up rentals. Like them, imagining the backcountry as my birthright, I kept wandering the hills above Winter Park and Fraser, searching for the solo ascent that could snap the world into focus and bring back that keen sense of home.

One morning I thought I might find it in the Byers Peak Wilderness, so I tossed a Nalgene and a bag of peanuts into my pack and set off for the trailhead. I had been staying at a bunkhouse in the Fraser Experimental Forest, where summer staff shared the kitchen and shower house with researchers from universities across the country. After elbowing my way to the sink to fill my water bottle in the crowded kitchen, I sighed with relief as I threw my gear into the back seat and crunched out onto the gravel road.

There were a few other cars parked at the trailhead in a dirt cul-de-sac looping around an island of subalpine fir, but I knew the elevation rose about 3,000 feet to the summit in just over four miles, which made for hard climbing. I still stood a good chance of having the peak to myself.

Winding through stands of lodgepole and spruce, sparse on the eastern slope, I thought about *Twin Peaks*, the David Lynch series I'd been watching after hours back at the bunkhouse. Following the murder of Laura Palmer, a hometown beauty with a wild side, federal agent Dale Cooper arrives in Twin Peaks to investigate. His unorthodox methods, which include transcendental meditation and standing on his head, blur distinctions between conscious and subconscious reality, and he discovers what the locals have known all along—that the woods, like Laura, harbor a darkness beneath the small-town charm. As I climbed, sweat speckling my brow, I wondered about all the hikers in Denver, what darkness they were trying to get away from as they drove up into the Rockies every weekend, why they all seemed so much like darkness to me. Maybe it's not a darkness in the woods, I thought, but a darkness in me, in us. Maybe we carry it with us wherever we go.

The steepness of the slope sliced into my thoughts as I climbed a series of switchbacks, and I began to concentrate on my breathing as I broke out onto an open ridge above the tree line. Most of the Byers Peak Wilderness is alpine country. The rocky path to the summit winds along a broad stretch of tundra, wispy clusters of grass spangled with bluebells and buttercups. In one of those meadows I caught four hikers, two men and two women well past middle age, who had stopped to rest on a jumble of boulders. All wore floppy fisherman's hats, and the women lifted their brims to smile at me as I passed, the men's faces in shadow as they sat with their elbows on their knees, one of them fiddling with a stem of grass. I felt a little lighter as I left them behind.

The ridge stretched up toward a rocky knob, a cornice falling over the western slope, and I saw two hikers moving slowly up the trail, a man and a girl. The man was tall and lanky, a red bandana knotted over his head, and the girl, maybe age ten, was struggling to keep up, sometimes falling onto her hands as her feet slid in the dirt and shale. Soon I reached them and asked to pass. The man turned and grinned, his teeth gleaming in his tanned face as he dropped a hand to the girl's shoulder. She stepped to the side and brushed her palms against the sides of her jeans as I lifted two fingers to my head in a half salute and continued on.

From there to the top I didn't see another soul, and I began to let my defenses down, gazing west over the valley where Fraser sat and north toward Rocky Mountain National Park. Snow cloaked many of the peaks I saw, running down avalanche chutes to glacial lakes. Clouds mounted on the horizon, thunder cells building to the east over the Front Range. I had climbed above 12,000 feet, and the air had noticeably thinned. My thoughts turned gauzy, lightened in part by the buzz I always got from a rigorous hike, and I grew a little euphoric as I neared the summit, my knees buckling as I lowered myself against a granite slab at the top. I sat there for many moments with my eyes closed, basking in the sun and the faint heat of the rock against my back, wind cooling my face as my eyelids glowed.

When I sat up, blinking, a mountain goat stood scarcely twenty yards away. My belly tingled with anticipation. The wind picked up and a clump of wool flapped out from its side. I could see bare patches along its back where it had been shedding. It might have been a billy or a nanny, since both have horns, but it looked thin and had a long beard, which likely meant it was male. At least that is how I thought of it, of him, the billy on the mountaintop.

Since I didn't see a mate or a goat kid nearby, I imagined he would be docile. Still, my thighs and arms tensed a bit as I faced him down. We stood like that for many moments, the goat blinking, his nostrils working as he raised his head. I was transfixed. There on that peak, adrenaline licking my ribs, I felt like the mountain's only child, granted this glimpse of the magical alpine realm.

The spell was quickly broken. The billy lowered his head as if fatigued and sidled my way with an idle interest. When he drew near enough for me to touch him, I could see his nose working again and a vacant look in his eye, like the gaze of a dog waiting for its dish to be filled. I thought of the cars parked at the trailhead and imagined the crowds that might scale the peak on the weekends, tossing bagels and apples to the goats and the mountain sheep. My mood darkened then, and I raised my arms. "Go on!" I yelled. "Get!" The billy jumped back a step, then ambled down the west side of the mountain, wool sagging from his back in long, dirty strips.

I turned on my heel, downcast, and began the descent, my belly hollow and cold. For a few moments, lying against the granite slab like I might have lounged as a child on my living room floor, I'd felt what I was yearning for, the old feeling that the way up was the way home. The billy heightened that fantasy, rising over the ridge like a birthday gift, yet he also brought a message I did not want to hear. Deep down I knew there was no going home, that all the time I spent climbing, thinking my eyes were trained on a lofty height, was really like walking backward, carried inexorably forward with my eyes fixed on the past. As I marched back toward the black blanket of the forest, skidding over the shale and leaping over washouts in the path, I lost interest in the view falling away on all sides, the green ridges rolling into blue, rain falling in gray sheets from clouds in the distance while the sun blazed overhead, the long sightlines out to the horizon where great peaks stood dwarfed against the sky. Soon I passed the other hikers still laboring up the ridgeline, and by the time I had reached my car the day might as well have been over, though it was early afternoon. I drove back to the bunkhouse, shut myself in my room, and read until evening fell.

———————

Ten years came and went. I moved to Nebraska for graduate school, returning to Idaho every summer to work in the Selway-Bitterroot Wilderness, and finally settled in Iowa, a landscape much like Uruguay's fertile plains.

I gave little thought to Byers Peak until I framed a photo I'd snapped of the billy on the summit, his coat blown sideways from his mangy back. As I centered the frame on the wall, remembering the little beggar trying to mooch a snack on the mountaintop, Sam's voice washed over the Colorado memory like a clean ray of light.

After a while, Sam said, *you stop looking for that mountaintop*. I can see his face wrinkling with a wry smile as he spoke, the sheep grazing on the hill beyond his shoulder, the wire fence around the *estancia* leaning as if it might collapse. And even though I can't be certain what Sam meant, I hear it now as a gentle reprimand. *Stop taking yourself so seriously*, I imagine him saying, if he'd continued his thought. *You can't live on the mountaintop.*

It's hard not to think in terms of mountaintops. This is the shape a story takes, building toward its climax, the way the body reaches and passes its prime. Our superlatives point upward, toward the apex or pinnacle, the height of experience. "She's at the top of her game," we say, or "He's reached his peak." For Buddhists and Hindus mountains are the dwelling places of the gods, reaching into the heavens, and according to Jewish tradition, God called Moses up the mountain and sent him down with the Ten Commandments. John Muir took this a step further by imagining mountains themselves as scripture. "Climb the mountains," he urged, "and get their good tidings."

These cultural leanings influenced my thirst for climbing as much as my sense of the summit as home. When Sam implied he'd given up looking for the mountaintop, I thought he'd gone dark inside, snuffed by all those years in the city, no longer reaching for the heights. But darkness as I imagine it now might also be seeing a solo climb as the only way to make the self whole. Even in Colorado, in the heart of the Rockies, the thrill of the peak felt fleeting because no matter how bright the day or how warm the stone against my back at the top, I knew the trail always led back down.

I still carry mountains with me as markers of who I am as a native Montanan, but for more than a decade I have lived in the Midwest, where the mountaintop does not exist and where living as if it does is a sure way to go mad with grief. And just as my sense of belonging on a mountain grew from the place where I woke and bathed and ate breakfast as a child, so it has changed as I've oriented myself within new space.

I am still working out my philosophy for living on the prairie, but the first principle is replacing the feeling that home is "up there" with the knowledge that it is "down here." There is no separation of peak and valley in the grasslands. Real life doesn't happen elsewhere—it's under my nose all the time. The "prairie eye," as Bill Holm would have it, watches for "horizontal grandeur, not vertical," relishing vastness far off and up close, gazing "at a square foot and [seeing] a universe." This is a landscape for the imagination, a subtle territory revealing nothing to those who make no effort to see, like a man who keeps his secrets close until he knows you really care. Among the grassy hills, where the shifting wind is stronger than gravity, where the knolls and hollows roll out like faces alone in a crowd, I am trying to listen to the place on its own terms. And if I were Sam, speaking to a young man who felt he might find what he was missing up on a granite peak, I'd say: You stop looking for the mountaintop when you realize you don't have to be on top of the world to see it clearly. After a while you realize being in the thick of it is enough.

The photograph of Byers Peak now sits in a closet, replaced by snapshots of an old green truck rusting near a wheat field, a close-up of an upright bass a friend made from a steel washtub and the wood of a cherry tree, and a row of men and women holding hands for a square dance on my wedding day. The nearest mountains are over a day's drive away, and I'm too busy canning beets and sweet cucumber pickles to worry much about what I might see from those distant peaks. The old urge to climb sometimes pushes me out on long bike rides along highways flanked by soybeans, yellow corn, and purple coneflowers, looping in a circle that always leads back to the garden, the smell of crushed garlic in the kitchen, my wife's laughter above the sizzle and snap of a stir-fry. These days I wake to the sun rising through the branches of the white pines in my front yard, brightening the oaks and maples and redbud trees down the street. Still a little heavy with sleep, I stagger into my running pants and lace up my shoes. I touch my toes a few times, yawning. Then, like a prairie dog, I step from my burrow into the early light, raise my arms, and stretch to my full height, which is as high as I need to be.

THIRTEEN

Circles

Central Iowa. Early May. Tomorrow is Mother's Day, when most gardeners in these parts begin planting seeds, trusting the last frost is past. I am kneeling in the dirt a day early, breathing the musky humus of the patch I have spaded up in the backyard as I transplant tomato and pepper seedlings, scooping a pit with one hand and steadying the root ball with the other as I fill in the edges. I am thinking of my mother and father, of the gardens we grew many years ago at the home place in Montana, where my father tilled an acre of the southern slope and we all walked the rows planting seeds. In one photograph of my sister and me at ages three and five, we squat along a furrow with our eyes fixed on the earth, ready to drop corn kernels from our carton of seeds into the finger holes we have made in the soil.

This is my first garden, at age thirty-three, the first plot I have cleared and hoed and planted myself. For many years I have been wandering, restless for flight every spring, heading north like the snow geese and angling west, hungry for streams swollen with snowmelt and booming with boulders rolling beneath the churning water. All that time I have never been rooted enough to grow anything. Until now Iowa has been the place I work, not the place I really live, the place I rise every morning with a foot out the door, ears and eyes cocked to the west.

No more: this summer I will stay. I have not chosen it. I yearn to be elsewhere, would be speeding away right now if I could. But I have been bracing myself for this since February, when the court summoned me for jury duty. In Marion County, I saw with dismay, this meant blocking off an entire month. It's not possible, I said to the clerk at the courthouse when I called. I have classes to teach. Not to worry, she said. We can defer you until summer. I sighed and said, Fine, it would have to be July. Thank you, Professor, she said. And that was that.

As I lowered the phone, it occurred to me I had been living in Iowa as if in exile for nearly five years. Part of this owed to the national love affair with the West, where filmmakers went for rapturous footage of Yosemite Falls, where it seemed most serious nature writers lived, and where I still aspired to return. I sometimes taught plains novels, Rølvaag, Sandoz, and Cather, reading the most lovely evocations aloud, like Jim Burden's sense of motion in the Nebraska landscape, which he felt "in the fresh, easy-blowing morning wind, and in the earth itself, as if the shaggy grass were a sort of loose hide, and underneath it herds of wild buffalo were galloping, galloping . . ." But even this was a paean to the past written from New York, where Cather lived for most of her adult life. It did not feel real to me as a way of seeing Nebraska or Iowa here and now. I needed more reasons than pioneers and the wild grasslands they plowed under to ground myself, my heart, my home in the prairie. The only thing worse than a summer of jury duty, I thought, would be a summer spent chafing against it. It was time to open my arms to the place, squint into the wind, and make an effort to see.

I bought a shovel and a hoe and began working the ground soon after it thawed, mounding each row so the roots could breathe in loose soil. I mooched seed potatoes from a friend, a few Yukon Gold and Colorado Rose, and let them sprout in a box under my bed as I watched and waited for Mother's Day.

I have been grading final essays all morning and need a break from the page, so I'm out in the backyard with my seedling trays, willing to gamble against a late frost. I'm glad for the sun on my face and neck. I feel the cool bosom of the earth against my knees, the grit building beneath my nails. The soil is damp, its scent sharp and fecund. I think of my grandfather as I plant a yellow pear tomato, one variety he always grew. I picture the bush in August laden with fruit. My mouth waters as I imagine sliding a golden tomato into my mouth, the skin firm against the inside of my cheek, warm from the sun. I can feel the juices explode as I burst the taut flesh, the acidic bite on my tongue, the sweet jelly pulp.

I finish my row of tomatoes and peppers and begin slicing spuds for the potato bed, taking care that each wedge I cut from the shriveled tuber has at least a sprout or two. As I bend once more to bury them, dreaming of the buttery taste of the Yukon Gold and the tender skin of the Colorado Rose, I see my father walking beside the tiller in Montana, wrestling the tines through the pale earth, bracing himself against the slope of the mountainside. He is shirtless and barefoot, wearing only bellbottom jeans, and his shoulders glisten with sweat, the ridges of his muscles rippling beneath his skin as he horses the tiller down the row, soil tumbling in a smooth ribbon behind him. I straighten along the potato row to rest my back, raising my arms with a yawn. When I bend again over the bed, digging with one cupped hand while lowering the tuber sprout into the hole, I see myself as a child watching my father's hands, gloveless, as mine are, planting seeds. My mother's father, too, worked the earth, coaxing yams and spinach and beets from the dry Idaho ground where he herded sheep. In a black-and-white Polaroid of my mother at age two, she peeks over the rim of a harvest basket as my grandfather carries her through the garden like an enormous head of cabbage.

I realize I am humming to myself as I plant a cucumber mound and two hills of butternut squash and a row of Red Ace beets, thinking I might add some basil and sage and sweet peas. It's a Greg Brown song running through my thoughts, one of his Iowa tunes, "Come and taste a little of the summer, my grandma put it all in jars." I am making mistakes, as I will learn in July while cutting back the tangled squash vines so the beets may breathe, but I am here, now, bone deep in this place. I do not think I have ever been so sure of my body, so driven by instinct, not even with a pack strapped to my back and my face set toward a snowy peak. My hands know without thinking what to do with these seeds. This knowledge washes over me like a burst of rain, that I have all the guides I need to see Iowa as it is. They are clamoring in my blood memory, all those gardeners on both sides marveling at this glacial loam. I remember how Jim Burden felt when he found Ántonia again after years apart. "I had the sense of coming home to myself," he said, "and of having found out what a little circle man's experience is." Iowa has been waiting for me all this time, under my feet, so much richer than the alkaline mountain soil my parents mixed every year with horse manure.

165

I know from a biologist friend that soil has horizons. The O horizon is organic residue on the surface, and the A horizon is topsoil, where seeds germinate. Deeper is the B horizon, subsoil, which provides structure for long roots, then the C horizon with loose minerals and stones, and finally the parent rock, which makes a mountain when pushed by a tectonic shift toward the sky. Through all the generations of earth-loving folk stretching back on both sides of my family tree, I begin to see how plunging my hands into this soil might help me, the grower, also take root.

———

Grades are in, graduation has come and gone, spring is turning to summer. The seeds are sprouting, thick shoots pushing up from the potato bed, cucumber and squash vines exploding from their little mounds, a perfect row of green beet tops straining sunward. Marigolds are said to ward off pests, so I transplant a few varieties in a ring around the edge of the plot. As I walk to the garden with my watering can, sprinkling a soft shower along each row, the soil darkens, water percolating into the earth.

Honking overhead. I look up. A gaggle of Canada geese in a V angles north and west. My chest swells with yearning, my feet itching for flight.

As I stand, tracking the geese, I hear a suckling sound at my feet. It is the gentlest of murmurs, so soft I think I've imagined it. But I get down on all fours with my ear to the ground and hear it again, a whisper rising out of the earth. My garden is drinking, I think. It is thirsty. At once I forget the geese, the wild north, the crags rising in the Black Hills and beyond. I fill the can again and watch the water arcing from the pinholes in the spout, soaking into the soil. I wonder if I am a little crazy for loving this patch of ground after only a few weeks, but it feels like an instinct, this hunger to cheer new life into being.

I buy a bale of straw and spread it over newspapers and cardboard I've laid between the rows to smother the weeds. It is a new method to me. In Montana my father tilled our entire garden patch and left the earth naked to the sun, carefully carving a trench along each row with a pointed hoe, banking loose dirt at the end for a reservoir. Then he ran a hose to the far end of the plot, where it was my job to water each trench. At first it was slow, the stream stumbling over loose clods and soaking into the freshly turned soil. But after I moistened each furrow once, I created a series of small riverbeds. In midsummer I watered each row six or seven times, watching the water dance down the channel as if I were a god gazing over a gorge, imagining rafters and kayakers shooting the rapids beneath a towering bank of green beans.

The straw will act as a mulch, holding moisture and shading the soil. It makes a gold ribbon around the whole plot, which I edge with a wire rabbit fence. When I leave for a conference in June, I think constantly of my plants, wondering if my neighbor is watering them as he promised. And when I come home, crunching back into the drive, it is hard not to break into a jog as I walk back to see the garden first thing. It's still there, the ring of marigolds blooming nicely in white and yellow and rusty red. The tomatoes and peppers have put on new leaves, and the purple potato blossoms are thick with honeybees.

Home. More than a mortgage, more than a mailbox, the native soil of the heart. I can feel the wheel of memory turning as I stand at the garden's edge, yet it no longer tugs my thoughts away from this place. Now it is spinning like the disc of the plow, turning the past underfoot, making it new. I can feel the soil of my heart loosening.

Late June. Afternoon. It is a sunny day, low eighties, with a strong southern wind. I walk my bicycle from the garage and prop it against the doorjamb. The clips on my shoes grind against the gravel as I adjust my helmet and chin strap, shrugging into a hydration pack and stuffing the hose down the front of my jersey. The bike is a blue-and-yellow road racer, built for short, stocky riders like me. I pinch the tires and pump a little air into the tubes. Then I clip in with one foot and swing my leg over the seat, easing down the gravel drive to the street.

It is a ritual now, a daily ceremony. When I wake every morning, I know I will ride, and before reading the news I look for the force and direction of the wind. I have learned the lesson the hard way, one day sailing effortlessly out twenty miles only to turn and struggle home into a headwind, moving so slowly through the heavy gusts it felt like I was standing still. There may be no mountains to climb, but I find wildness and solitude on the bike, coasting through the deserted campus, the dorms fallen quiet and dark.

I feel the wind on one cheek as I pedal east to the edge of town. When I turn south, it surges into my face, over my arms, against my legs. Wind is a stubbornness, a resistance I can sense but not see, one of the great facts of the plains. Those who have gazed upon empty fields thinking them barren have never cycled into the wind. It is a power known only by its effects. I can understand why so many of the preachers I heard as a child described the spirit as a rushing wind. As a gust hits my chest, wobbling my front tire, I too must believe in the unseen.

The road south of town dips into a series of hills, and I work the sprocket to full torque on the downslope, hunched over the handlebars on the lookout for potholes. I coast up the incline and stand on the pedals when my momentum slows, shifting down as I grow short of air, my thighs burning as I roll over the steep crest, into the wind. I go through the gears down another descent, then pump my way up the next hill. I need this fire in my chest, these smoldering thighs. The old wanderlust will not die easily.

As I sweep down the last hill and turn at a fork in the road, I hit a long flat angling south and west. The wind shifts to the other side of my face. I gear down and settle in, my feet like two dancers spinning in time. The long open stretch gives me time to take note of the sky, a scatter of cirrus blown over the blue overhead. A raptor wheels in the distance above a field where a tractor pulls a white tank through the corn.

I think of a phone call the day before. A woman from New York whom I want to meet. A woman who works in magazines. I heard of her soon after she moved to Des Moines, and we have been writing for a week while she is traveling on business, introducing ourselves, flirting toward a first date. I carried my phone out to the garden the past afternoon, my hands unsteady as I rang her cell. She answered from the back of a cab. She asked me to wait, and I heard the slam of the door and the cabbie's voice as she asked for change. Then she was back, heels clicking down the sidewalk as a bus groaned away from the curb. She laughed when I said I was standing in my garden. It sounds lovely, she said. We made lunch plans for the following week.

I should know better by now than to trust the gut ache of the crush I feel building as I read her messages each day, but it washes back over my belly, mingled with the dull pain in my legs as I spin over the asphalt. I cross a river, pass an aggregate mine where trucks haul away limestone, gravel, and sand, and turn west on a newly paved highway. The shoulder is wider here, shielded from traffic by rumble bars, and I ease into reverie as the tires hum over the road, my body rocking on the saddle. Purple coneflowers rise along the fencerows. Black-eyed Susans and mullein and, near one farm, a cluster of hollyhocks. I smile, recalling that these flowers were once meant to mark the outdoor privy, so visiting ladies would not need to ask where it was.

I take the exit to Knoxville and turn north, riding in traffic past a football stadium with a stone gate. Home of the Panthers, it says. I wonder if panthers roamed among the mammoths and bison and elk when the land was a great sea of grass. I dodge an opening car door downtown, cycling past the limestone courthouse on Main Street, then east up the hill out of town. Farms all the way to the Red Rock Dam, cows and sheep, corn and beans. Then another sweep north, when I feel the tailwind catch my back as I climb the hill above the dam, hammering over the crest and sailing down twenty, twenty-five, thirty-five miles an hour. A crosswind gusts up the river channel. Pelicans spiral over the spillway, skating to a stop on the water, paddling through the jetsam to gulp carp stunned by the turbines.

I'm too tired for thinking now. I cross the dam and cruise down the homestretch. The wind carries me across an overpass, and I stand in the pedals to climb the last hill, rolling to a stop in the gravel drive, swinging a leg over the saddle, clipping out.

The ritual has achieved its design. Flight and return. I walk gingerly into the house for water and carry it out to a hammock chair by the garden and drink my fill and close my eyes against the sun. The breeze cools my face. I imagine my route on a map, the loop east, south, west, north, and home. I can still feel the hum of the wheels, the dance of my feet, sprockets spinning and spinning, their teeth tugging the links in the chain.

———————

First day of July. I call the courthouse and learn the docket is clear for the week. The garden is raucous with blossoms and shoots. I have been making pasta with fresh basil and sage, salads with beet tops and cucumbers and peas. The potato bed is now a tall mound where I raked up more earth on both sides to cover the base of the vines. The squash blossoms are great golden blooms I can nearly hear booming open in the midmorning sun, when the bees flock in, jostling each other for a chance at the stamen, brawling deep in the blossom then weaving away, drunken it seems. I lose an hour just standing there, as transfixed as I've ever been by the crackling dance of a fire.

In a few days I fill a brown grocery bag with sweet peas and a bunch each of basil and sage and drive to Des Moines to meet the woman from New York. I park at the Art Center, a stark white building with modern angles and cubes on all sides but the back, where a limestone wall opens into a rose garden and park. I'm early, so I walk through the park to quiet myself. It's shady there beneath the great elms and oaks. I linger for a moment beside a Goldsworthy cairn, a great cone of limestone balanced between two stone blocks, each with the shape of the cairn cut into its face. I think of echoes, of seeds, of the curve of an egg. I remember wilderness cairns, benchmarks of balanced rock along faint mountain trails to remind me I was on the right path.

I carry my bag of peas and herbs into the restaurant and reserve a table for two. The walk has steadied me, yet fear still burns in my chest. I have always disliked the pageantry of the first date, the chitchat, the high stakes. I would do better at a barn dance, swinging my partner over the boards and the straw. I would do better with music and beer and friends at my side.

The thought of the garden grounds me as I wait. I am thinking of fresh tomatoes in August, the juice of a ripe Brandywine, when she arrives. I know her from pictures, the curly cascade of her hair, the gleam of her smile. I stand and wave. She grins and shoulders her purse and walks my way. Before we sit, I give her the bag. Sweet peas, I say. And basil and sage. She opens it and lowers her face and breathes. My family is from Italy, she says. My great-grandfather gardened in the city, in Philly, after he came over, and he always smelled like basil. I smile, and we sit, and the knot in my chest begins to unclench.

After lunch we walk through the park, past the cairn, beneath the cool sweep of trees. In a few years we will be married here on a hot July afternoon, but we don't know that yet. We are quiet, and my belly burns again with nerves. We stop to admire a yellow rose, and she bends to breathe its soft scent. We wander the path silently. When we reach our cars, I'm not sure if I will see her again. I offer a hug and say I hope she'll let me know what she thinks of the peas. She smiles and says she must go. As I drive home, I think of her dark hair against my cheek, of the smell of coconut and honey in the lotion she wore.

Saturday. Ninety degrees at Lake Red Rock. A breeze blows in from the cove as we smooth a cloth over a picnic table and unpack the food. She has brought hummus-and-cheese sandwiches wrapped in foil, and I have two fresh cucumbers, scrubbed and trimmed at the ends. She loved the peas, she says. I say I am glad. The silence feels right this time as we unwrap the sandwiches and eat, gazing out at the lake. The hummus is soft and delicious with the cheese, a goat *chèvre* from a local dairy. There is arugula in the sandwich from the farmers market, the bread from a bakery downtown.

I tell her that a friend likes to say Iowa has everything you need to survive. She laughs and says that sounds a little extreme. But it's true, I insist. You can grow almost anything, and with a few goats and a clean well, you'd be set. She chuckles. Are you planning to raise your own goats? Maybe, I say. They're pretty good composters.

After lunch we walk along the water's edge, stepping carefully from stone to stone. We find a flat rock and bask for a spell in the sun, our eyes closed against the light. When I sit up, squinting against the glare on the lake, I see her gazing past the mouth of the cove at the sailboats drifting in from the marina on the far shore. She is wearing a blue floral top, propped on her hands, and I think it would be a perfect time to lean in, touch her cheek.

But I can't do it yet. *Never apologize,* I tell myself, firmly. *Flounder and flop all you want, but never explain.*

When our arms fall asleep and the sun grows too hot, we stand, stiffly, and walk back to our cars. Another hug. Once more with the downcast eyes and shy grins. I promise to call. Please do, she says. And I drive home thinking next time I will summon the nerve.

As I crank on the faucet and soak the straw mulch, I think at my age I should know what to say, what to do, how to move, but I have never mastered the opening dance. I am still, at heart, a shy country rube. I ease up on the nozzle to soften the stream, showering the beets and squash and potatoes. The straw darkens beneath the water. I breathe deeply of grass and damp soil and the musk of tomato leaves.

———————

I call the courthouse on Monday and learn I must appear for jury selection the next day. So I cinch up a tie and shrug into a jacket and drive to Knoxville, the county seat. It's the reverse of my ride, since I loop through from the south to catch the wind coming back, but it is familiar country now, the dam at the lake, the pelicans, the land rolling away in straight lines of green corn. Grant Wood comes to mind, and then I think of the organic farms springing up, the vegetable bins at the market downtown, eight kinds of potatoes, rainbow chard, red and green and dinosaur kale. It's not all fencerows and combines anymore, I think. There's a little wildness creeping back.

I park at the limestone courthouse and climb the stairs and slide into a wooden bench in the gallery with the other potential jurors. We are a furtive bunch, come here because we must. The bailiff bustles in, a woman with permed hair and a dress suit, heels clicking over the floor. As she starts to read from her roster, I am suddenly nine years old again, gazing longingly toward the window in hope of recess. I shake myself back to the room, wondering who is on trial and why, reminding myself that both sides are trusting us to be fair-minded and just.

Then the two legal teams take their places, and we file into the jury box and stand as the judge climbs his bench. We see the accused, a tall middle-aged man, and hear the charges against him. His eyes are wide, his dark hair gleaming with gel. He is an immigrant, his lawyer informs us, in search of the American Dream. And we are all white. I feel nauseous. The prosecuting attorney is a friendly looking woman who asks us if we can be persuaded, beyond doubt, solely by his alleged victim's word. In this case, she says, it is as if a parent put a cake by the door and told three children to leave it alone and then discovered finger swipes through it, and only one child with frosting smeared on his mouth. It's that simple, she says. The defense lawyer is a tall, beefy man with nearly translucent skin. We can see the blood rise and subside in his cheeks. Reasonable doubt, he assures us, is no simple matter. It is like leaping from an airplane with a parachute.

Before you do, you want to know who packed the chute, whether there is a backup in case the first rip cord fails. You want to be stone sure, he says. You hold a man's good name in your hands.

It takes nearly an hour, and each attorney singles us out, calling our names, searching our faces. I am not certain I can surpass reasonable doubt based on the plaintiff's word, alone, I say to the prosecution. To the defense, I reveal that my students have written personal accounts of the violence the man is charged with. In the end neither side deems me fit, and I am released. The clerk thanks me as I leave. Please call again on Monday, she says.

The summer heat hits my face as I walk through the door. I loosen my tie and take a deep breath. My heart lifts a little to be free of that place. But on the drive home I think of the man sitting ramrod straight in his chair, fear etched into his face. I think of the woman he might have battered, and since I do not know what is true, I ache for us all.

I ready the bike first thing when I'm home. The wind is easterly, so I ride through town and out past the pool and the megachurch, its high windows blue with the sky. I stand on the pedals as I approach a hog lot, nearly retching as I speed away. The reek of the hogs is nearly as strong as the wind. It's a long, hilly stretch out to New Sharon and back, some thirty-four miles, and I keep standing from the saddle to grind away until my legs turn to jelly, gasping as I strain against the handlebars and finally lower myself to the seat. My thoughts turn fuzzy with fatigue, and I need the tailwind to carry me home.

My knees nearly buckle as I clip out. I carry cold water to the chair in the yard, where the squash blossoms are buzzing with bees, and I drink so quickly my head throbs. When the pain subsides, I gulp again, greedily. I sink into the chair, but I cannot sleep. I think of the man in the courtroom. I imagine the woman weeping as she takes the stand. My back knots up from the ride, my shoulders cramping against the backrest. I stand and walk inside and stay in the shower until the water turns cold.

Saturday. Low nineties and breezy. I have been boiling fresh beets. My face speckles with sweat as I slip off their skins and set them in separate bowls with a wedge of butter to melt in the steam. My mouth waters as I imagine

173

the clean, earthy flavor and sweet aftertaste of the Red Ace. I hear her car in the driveway and look out the kitchen window over the sink. She is wearing a white dress with red and orange flowers embroidered on the neck and the hem. Her hair hangs freely over her shoulders, her arms bare, her toes smiling from the lip of her sandals.

For a moment I see her like that as she walks toward me, her face soft in the afternoon sun. I feel the cramp in my chest loosen. Each time we have talked new depths have opened, as if we are walking through the old Iowa prairie, grass over our heads, parting the stalks with our hands without ever reaching the edge.

This time when I say hello and sweep her into a hug, I sense we have traveled beyond the opening moves, past the chess match of doubting what's next. This time I am here, all of me, pretenses aside. She sets a peach cobbler on the countertop. It fills the kitchen with the smell of warm sugar and oatmeal. We make a spinach salad, and she whips up a dressing with balsamic vinegar, oil, Dijon mustard, and garlic while I grate a little cheese. It's too late for peas, I say with a shrug. So sad, she says, I can never eat too many peas.

I spread a quilt over the grass by the garden, and we make a few trips with the food. When I go back to the house the last time, I uncork a bottle of wine. She asks where the quilt came from. It's a bear claw pattern, I say. My mother made it from old corduroy. I love to quilt, she says. It slows me down. One of my great-grandfathers was a tailor in Philly, and my grand-mom on the other side loved to sew. I like making things.

I motion toward the garden and say I understand. She smiles. The potatoes vines are still blooming, though the purple flowers have thinned. A hole gapes in the tomato row where I lost a Golden Treasure to wilt. In a few weeks the first yellow pear fruit will ripen, then the first Brandywines. We can see little green peppers at the ends of the stems. The squash vines have climbed the fence and spread over the yard, the broad leaves lifted skyward like strong, generous hands.

We sit quietly in the shade drinking wine. The quilt smells of cotton and grass. I am thinking of circles, of the happy chance of our meeting. What were the odds, I say, of me finding you here? She smiles, her eyes closed in the breeze.

It would look like a mess on a map, my migrations from Montana to Tennessee to Nebraska, then Uruguay, Colorado, Nebraska, Idaho, and Iowa, looping back west every summer. And she left New Jersey for California, wheeling east to North Carolina then Philly then Senegal, finally New York, where her magazine closed and she heard of the job in Des Moines. Call it fate or the doodling hand of chance, we might never have met if not for the court summons and a whole chain of happenstance.

We finish the wine and lie back. I lift my arms, propping my head in my hands. The earth curves against my spine, the smell of soil mingling with the grass. I think of planting seeds, how quickly the motion came back to me. *All this time,* I wonder, *can it be that the place has been planting me?*

I turn and reach for her hand. Her hair spills over the quilt, dark against the red and tan corduroy. As I pull her to me and feel the heat of her breath and smell the honey lotion on her skin, it is as if I am also drawn in, the way the seed and the soil share one need.

———————

Twice more I call the courthouse, but each time the docket is clear. And then it is August and I am released, and I eat the first ripe yellow pear, juicy and tart between my teeth. The plant towers over me, nearly eight feet where I have staked up the vines. I bury my face in its leaves and breathe and breathe. When the potato vines turn brown in their hill, I borrow a digging fork from a friend and ease it under the mound, breaking the soil, the spuds spilling out, clumps of dirt clinging to the golden and rose-colored skins. I think of roasting them in wedges with rosemary and oil until they puff and pillow in the heat. The cucumber vines lie withered on the compost pile. The peppers are thickening, and I bend near the Brandywine plant to admire the green fruit bulging beneath the leaves. The squash will surge well into the fall.

She comes to visit before I head north for a few days with friends, planning to paddle all day and camp in the pines at night, my clothes soaking up the smoke of the fire. This time when I kiss her goodbye, I leave the house craving not only the going out, but also the turning back, the return. And all week in the woods I think of her, of the garden, of the silty loam of that place. When I lie awake at night listening to loons keening on the water, I remember the quilt and the wine and the green smell of grass. I paddle all day in peace because I am not fighting time. *This life is good*, I think, *and that life is good, and the two are one life, two halves of one ring.*

Then we break camp, and I am glad to drive south. When I surface from the forest onto the plains, wind buffets the car like the firm hand of a headwind against my face on a long ride. I can sense my center shifting. I will always hear the mountains' wild call as my parent rock, but now I also know the horizons of soil, how they swaddle the earth, how the richest dirt lies near my feet, where every spring the seeds are sustained by decay and by sun and by rain.

I have been thinking of growth, I will tell her when I park at her place. I am open to growth, I will say. Her eyes will glisten as she draws me close. And with my head on her shoulder, my face in her hair, she will hold me and ask me to stay.

It is a warm Sunday morning in April, just before sunrise. I am running a bike path along a shaded creek, waving away gnats swarming from the backwater. I will finish with a sprint, but today's route covers twelve miles, so for now I hold back and focus and breathe. The asphalt rolls out before me in the half-light of dawn. My chest rises and falls to the beat of my feet.

My wife and I live in Des Moines in a brick house built for coalminers a half century ago. Coneflowers, hostas, and hollyhocks rim the backyard. I have planted two apple trees, a Newtown Pippin and a Jonathan, and by the time I set out this year's Brandywines and Sweet Italian peppers our first child, a girl, will have been born. We have been trying out family names since Christmas: Sophia, Luisa, Elisabeth. Lately we've been thinking of Linden, the national tree of the Czech Republic, known for its fragrant blossoms and its talent, as legend would have it, for bursting into song.

Such a perilous task, this naming, so easy to mistake ourselves for authors when we'll really be readers and editors, trying to let our daughter's best story unfold. I think of my own name, Joshua, how my parents believed it would mark me as a standard bearer for faith, how many years it has taken to shed the weight of that hope. But it is hard not to project my own thoughts on my girl. I can't help imagining her lovely and brilliant and kind.

This much I know. I am lucky to have found love. When I finish a run, I am glad to see our sturdy house beneath the white pines towering over the yard. I like waking up with my wife to the smell of those pines drifting through the window. This year as I wait for my daughter's birth I will plant Mayan corn along the fence and train Speckled Cranberry beans to climb the cornstalks. I will lend a hand for a day at the farm where we buy fresh eggs, pulling weeds among the lettuce and radishes, listening to the rustle of orb weavers spinning their webs in the edges of the hoop house.

This is rich life, neither higher nor lower, the right kind of soil for my daughter's first steps. I want her to know the pleasure of sowing, reaching down to the warm earth with a seed and watching it grow—one way I have found to make any place home. A friend says all gardeners must be optimists, and though I also turn a wary eye to thunderheads, staking tomatoes from all sides to keep them upright in high winds, I think he is right. A garden is a risk worth taking, like the choice I want to make as a father to keep moving beyond inevitable mistakes, toward the sun at its zenith and on toward the waning light.

My breath is even and slow as my feet drum on the planks of a bridge at the halfway mark. I force down some gel as I cross the Raccoon River. The water laps at the bank, brown and swollen with rain. The sun has climbed above the treetops. My face burns with blood. I squeeze a few drops of water over my head. I know euphoria will set in at mile eight, my thoughts fizzing like a fresh glass of seltzer, but for now I feel calm. Canada geese stand along the shore preening themselves, pecking at the grass, stretching to their full height and beating their wings without ever leaving the ground. I catch a small second wind, as if a chamber is thrown open in my chest. My heart rate slows. For a moment I am nearly free of sensation. Sweat cools the back of my neck. I round the turn at a bend in the river and head home.

All this running, so much straining into the wind. Even in winter, when I strap rubber tracks laced with wire to my shoes, I need a little danger to know I am alive. It is a way to find wilderness in the middle of town, tiptoeing over black ice beneath streetlights as frost forms on my jacket, the houses dark, every block desolate. I run for the bliss and the pain, for the flame in my lungs as much as the afterglow. And sometimes I run to forget.

The trail curves back toward an overpass where traffic drones on the interstate, and my thoughts drift across the plains toward Montana. My head bubbles with runner's ecstasy. I imagine driving the route with my wife and our baby, the pilgrimage to the high country. I know the old melancholy will creep back soon enough, but I don't feel it now. I am just traveling with my girls along the Clark Fork, toward the snowy Cabinet Mountain peaks, through the Bull River Valley to the sea-green waters of the Kootenai. I pick up the pace, my heart pounding as I fight for breath.

The last mile rolls through a wrinkle of hills in our neighborhood, where limestone ranches and brick bungalows rest beneath the sugar maples and elms. Fire creeps into my thighs, my belly, rising beneath my ribs. I forget the road west, all those aching years, and I need no more wildness for this moment than the truth of my searing lungs. It is no longer penance, nor freedom or flight. I race the last leg of my loop because I want to get back to the pines and the house and my wife. It is a spring morning in Iowa, nearly past the last frost, and my garden lies waiting beneath the straw mulch and leaves. My daughter is kicking in the womb, restless to get on with her life. I can't wait to meet her, to show her all of my love. I don't want to miss anything, so I gasp up the last hill, angle into the side street, and dig as deep as I can down the block toward my home.

ACKNOWLEDGMENTS

Above all I am grateful to my wife, Amy, for believing in this book and for helping me discover home. I thank my parents for their love and support, Ted Kooser for teaching me restraint, Keith Ratzlaff and Walter Cannon for their encouragement, Carol Roh Spaulding and Timothy Bascom for their careful reading, and Joshua Pomeroy for his friendship and honesty. I am also grateful to Central College for a yearlong sabbatical, without which this project might have been delayed for many years.

Finally, I am indebted to the editors of the following journals, in which portions of these chapters first appeared in different form: "Uruguay" in *Ascent*; "Selway by Headlamp" in *Fourth Genre*; "Prelude" (formerly "The Shallows and the Deeps") in *The Gettysburg Review*; "The Shadow of the Kootenai" in *Hotel Amerika*; "Down from the Mountaintop" in *ISLE*; "Alberta" in *The Kenyon Review*; and "The Sweet Spot" in *Shenandoah*.